Foundations for Eternal Life

Things We Know • Things We Do
Things God Does

By Thomas G. Edel

...like a tree planted by streams of water...

Psalm 1

Foundations for Eternal Life

Things We Know • Things We Do
Things God Does

By Thomas G. Edel

A free download of this book may be available at
ShalomKoinonia.org

Send comments & suggestions for revision to:
Thomas@ShalomKoinonia.org

Table of Contents

Preface

"Come to me, all who labor and are heavy laden, and I will give you rest. Take my yoke upon you, and learn from me, for I am gentle and lowly in heart, and you will find rest for your souls. For my yoke is easy, and my burden is light."
Matthew 11:28-30

"If anyone thirsts, let him come to me and drink. Whoever believes in me, as the Scripture has said, 'Out of his heart will flow rivers of living water.'" John 7:37-38

Jesus invites each of us to come to him. This is an invitation to salvation: *"Come to me."* Salvation is not primarily a matter of things we know, or things we do; salvation is a matter of right relationship:

> *"And this is eternal life, that they know you the only true God, and Jesus Christ whom you have sent."* John 17:3

Eternal life involves knowing God; having right relationship with God. In order to know God better, we should learn things and do things that strengthen our relationship with God. We should avoid things that hurt our relationship with God. That is the point of writing about *"Things We Know,"* *"Things We Do,"* and *"Things We Should NOT Do."* The goal is to know God better; to deepen our relationship with God; to deepen our love for God.

Have you already come to Jesus? If so, may this book help you deepen your relationship with God.

Have you not yet come to Jesus? May this book help you begin your relationship with God.

> *The Spirit and the bride say, "Come!" And let him who hears say, "Come!" Whoever is thirsty, let him come; and whoever wishes, let him take the free gift of the water of life.* Revelation 22:17 NIV

****

Foundations for Eternal Life 5

Introduction

Confusion about spiritual things is widespread. Spiritual confusion produces broken lives. This book attempts to clarify important spiritual truth, so that clarity will overcome confusion, so that broken lives will be made whole.

The purpose of this book is **not** to present new insight, but rather to present old truth in a clear and simple way for easy understanding.

This book covers many important topics. Other authors have written whole books on topics that are covered here in just a couple pages. Don't expect exhaustive coverage of any topic; but do expect a lot to be covered in a few pages.

I have tried to limit the material to subjects that:

- have very strong and clear scriptural support, and
- apply to all people in all cultures.

May the words on these pages help you know God's love for you, understand God better, and love God deeply.

I encourage you to make the following prayer your own:

O God, help me to know your love for me.

Help me to learn your ways, and to walk in them.

Open my spiritual eyes to see myself as you see me, and to understand my circumstances as you understand them.

Fill me with your Spirit so that I will be able to follow you wherever you lead.

Did you mean it? Or, was that prayer just empty words? What would it take for you to mean that prayer?

Consider praying that prayer for real.

****

Ways to Use this Book

The order that subjects are presented in this book is significant, so **it would be good to read this book straight through.**

However, if you don't have time to read the whole book, you may prefer to **pick a topic of interest in the Table of Contents and start there.** Do what works for you!

Each chapter is fairly short, so this book can easily be used as a **daily devotional**, for those who would benefit from that.

This book can also be used to facilitate **small group discussion or study.** Pick topics that interest the group for as many meetings as seems beneficial. It may work well to simply take turns reading through a chapter and discussing the referenced verses and any questions included. The discussion could revolve around a simple ongoing question: **"What about you? How should this affect you?"** Chapters are arranged to facilitate printing or copying one chapter at-a-time, so each group member can have a copy. Per the copyright notice at the front of this book, **this book may be freely copied and freely distributed.**

In keeping the chapters short, there is a great deal that is left unsaid. For those who want to go deeper, each chapter ends with suggestions **"For Further Reflection."** These are usually scripture references, and sometimes a few questions. If you have time, **you will likely benefit by looking into scripture for deeper truth** (and to verify or disprove what is written in this book). Sometimes another book is referenced. Some of the best books I have read are not well-known; perhaps my recommendations will benefit you.

Keep in mind that all books other than scripture are flawed, since they are written by imperfect people. Ask God for discernment between truth and error as you read these pages.

****

PART 1
Things We Know

Throughout the letters of the New Testament, the emphasis is first on things we should **KNOW.** Then the emphasis turns to things we should **DO.** **Right thinking** generally comes before **right actions.** We cannot **live** in a way that is pleasing to God if we don't first learn to **think** in a way that is pleasing to God.

So, the emphasis in Part 1 of this book is on things we should **KNOW.** Part 2 will turn the focus to things we should **DO.**

****

Chapter 1
In the Beginning, God

In the beginning, God created the heavens and the earth.
Genesis 1:1

Oh give thanks to the LORD, for he is good,
for his steadfast love endures forever!
Psalm 107:1

There is a God, one God, who created the heavens and the earth, and everything in them. You are part of his creation. Though you already may know that, it is worth reviewing, as there are many who deny the existence of God, or who believe in a god who is much different than the God who *"created the heavens and the earth"* and whose *"steadfast love endures forever."*

Scripture doesn't spend much time arguing for God's existence. Followers of Jesus generally understand that God has revealed himself in scripture and in creation, and it appears that God doesn't think he needs to spend time establishing his own existence. Rather, scripture says such things as:

The fool says in his heart, "There is no God."
Psalm 14:1, Psalm 53:1

For since the creation of the world God's invisible qualities—his eternal power and divine nature—have been clearly seen, being understood from what has been made, so that men are without excuse. Romans 1:20 NIV

In the beginning, God created the heavens and the earth. Genesis 1:1

If you find yourself struggling regarding the existence of God, this may be partly due to:

- A daily media barrage opposing true belief.

- The hypocrisy of many who claim to follow God.
- Peer pressure to not believe in God.
- Your own wrong beliefs about God, such as blaming God for all the evil in the world and in your life.
- Previous negative experiences with "church."

How much do each of the above points influence you?

To the extent possible for you, turn the media barrage down; don't let hypocrites keep you from the truth; don't follow your peers to hell; acknowledge that some of your beliefs about God may be wrong; **don't let the failures of others keep you from eternal life!**

To truly know God, it is important that you seek him with **all your heart.** For God has said:

> *"You will seek me and find me when you seek me with all your heart."*   Jeremiah 29:13

Many people fail in their pursuit of God precisely at this point. They don't really seek to know God and follow him. Rather, what they really want is a supernatural being, like Santa Claus or a genie, who will simply give them what they want without expecting anything in return.

What about you? Do you really want to know and follow God, or just find a genie to make your problems go away?

For Further Reflection

Acts 17:24-28: Paul speaking in Athens about the Creator.

Hebrews 11:3: The universe formed by God's word.

Genesis 1:1 to 2:3: The seven days of creation.

1Corinthians 8:4-6: Explaining about one God.

John 8:31-32: Knowing the truth will set you free.

Book Reference: "Beneath Foundations for Eternal Life" by Thomas Edel. Free ebook available at ShalomKoinonia.org.

****

Chapter 2
In the Beginning Was the Word

In the beginning was the Word, and the Word was with God, and the Word was God. He was in the beginning with God. All things were made through him, and without him was not any thing made that was made. In him was life, and the life was the light of men. … And the Word became flesh and dwelt among us… John 1:1-4, 14

He said to them, "But who do you say that I am?" Simon Peter replied, "You are the Christ, the Son of the living God." Matthew 16:15-16

———————

What about you? Who do you say Jesus is?

In writing this chapter, I had difficulty coming up with any words of my own that accurately clarify scripture. So, on the topic of who Jesus is, here are some important verses:

Again the high priest asked him, "Are you the Christ, the Son of the Blessed One?"
"I am," said Jesus. "And you will see the Son of Man sitting at the right hand of the Mighty One and coming on the clouds of heaven." Mark 14:61-62 NIV(see also Daniel 7:13-14)

"Therefore let all Israel be assured of this: God has made this Jesus, whom you crucified, both Lord and Christ." Acts 2:36 NIV

He is the image of the invisible God, the firstborn of all creation. For by him all things were created, in heaven and on earth, visible and invisible, whether thrones or dominions or rulers or authorities—all things were created through him and for him. And he is before all things, and in him all things hold together. And he is the head of the body, the church. He is the beginning, the firstborn from the dead, that in everything he might be preeminent. Colossians 1:15-18

Have this mind among yourselves, which is yours in Christ Jesus, who, though he was in the form of God, did not count equality with God a thing to be grasped, but made himself nothing, taking the form of a servant, being born in the likeness of men. And being found in human form, he humbled himself by becoming obedient to the point of death, even death on a cross. Therefore God has highly exalted him and bestowed on him the name that is above every name, so that at the name of Jesus every knee should bow, in heaven and on earth and under the earth, and every tongue confess that Jesus Christ is Lord, to the glory of God the Father. Philippians 2:5-11

"You know the message God sent to the people of Israel, telling the good news of peace through Jesus Christ, who is Lord of all." Acts 10:36 NIV

And Jesus came and said to them, "All authority in heaven and on earth has been given to me." Matthew 28:18

Jesus did many other miraculous signs in the presence of his disciples, which are not recorded in this book. But these are written that you may believe that Jesus is the Christ, the Son of God, and that by believing you may have life in his name. John 20:30-31 NIV

These verses indicate that Jesus is **the Christ**, **the Son of God**, **Lord of all**. He was **"in the form of God"** before his life on earth, and **"by him all things were created"**!

For Further Reflection

What do the terms "Christ," "Lord" and "Son of God" mean? Is Jesus one of many christs, or is Jesus the only true Christ?

Luke 1:31-35: The angel Gabriel's words to Mary.

John 8:21-59: Why don't you understand?

1Corinthians 8:4-6: Explaining about one God.

Hebrews 1:1-14: God has spoken to us by his Son.

Book Reference: "The Case for Christ" by Lee Strobel.

****

Chapter 3
Sin Entered the World

And the LORD God commanded the man, saying, "You may surely eat of every tree of the garden, but of the tree of the knowledge of good and evil you shall not eat, for in the day that you eat of it you shall surely die."   Genesis 2:16-17

Therefore, just as sin entered the world through one man, and death through sin, and in this way death came to all men, because all sinned...   Romans 5:12 NIV

Why is there so much evil in the world? This question is answered in Genesis chapter 3, where Adam and Eve disobeyed God, thereby bringing sin and death into the world. Everyone descended from Adam and Eve is affected. As scripture says:

If we say we have no sin, we deceive ourselves, and the truth is not in us.   1John 1:8

If we say we have not sinned, we make him a liar, and his word is not in us.   1John 1:10

...for all have sinned and fall short of the glory of God...   Romans 3:23

Generally speaking, "sin" may be defined as any thought or action that violates God's moral law. (God is the ultimate judge of what is right or wrong; this should be self-evident.)

The main consequence of sin is death:

For the wages of sin is death...   Romans 6:23

...death spread to all men because all sinned... Rom. 5:12

I understand that the "death" referred to here has both a physical and a spiritual component. We physically die a natural death because of sin, and we are all spiritually dead prior to receiving new life through Christ. This spiritual death is referred to elsewhere in scripture, such as:

As for you, you were dead in your transgressions and sins... Ephesians 2:1 NIV

And you, who were dead in your trespasses and the uncircumcision of your flesh... Colossians 2:13

Moreover, because God is completely righteous and holy, our sin separates us from God:

...but your iniquities have made a separation between you and your God, and your sins have hidden his face from you so that he does not hear. Isaiah 59:2

We may try to justify ourselves by reasoning that our good deeds somehow compensate for our bad deeds, but that is not how scripture views it:

For whoever keeps the whole law and yet stumbles at just one point is guilty of breaking all of it. James 2:10 NIV

The prophet Isaiah said it well:

For our offenses are many in your sight, and our sins testify against us. Our offenses are ever with us, and we acknowledge our iniquities: rebellion and treachery against the LORD, turning our backs on our God, fomenting oppression and revolt, uttering lies our hearts have conceived. Isaiah 59:12-13 NIV

What about you? Do you claim that you have not sinned?

In what ways have you rebelled against God?

What are the consequences of your sins?

For Further Reflection

Genesis 3:1-24: The fall of man / the first sin.

Luke 18:9-14: The Pharisee and the tax collector.

Romans 3:9-20: There is no one righteous.

Psalm 51: King David's confession of sin.

****

Chapter 4
Christ Died for Our Sins

For I delivered to you as of first importance what I also received: that Christ died for our sins in accordance with the Scriptures, that he was buried, that he was raised on the third day in accordance with the Scriptures... 1Corinth. 15:3-4

For while we were still weak, at the right time Christ died for the ungodly. For one will scarcely die for a righteous person—though perhaps for a good person one would dare even to die—but God shows his love for us in that while we were still sinners, Christ died for us. Romans 5:6-8

For Christ also suffered once for sins, the righteous for the unrighteous, that he might bring us to God... 1Peter 3:18

In the Old Testament, under the Law of Moses, a religious system based on rules and regulations was established by God. The Law of Moses was not God's ultimate plan for salvation, but was a temporary system intended to expose and punish sin, and to promote true faith by doing so. It also provided a legal system for the people of Israel, fulfilling a similar purpose as the various legal systems in countries throughout the world today. A primary purpose of the Law of Moses was to lead the people to true faith:

So the law was put in charge to lead us to Christ that we might be justified by faith. Galatians 3:24 NIV

As part of the Law of Moses a system of animal sacrifices was set up, which showed the need for blood sacrifice to deal with people's sins. However, the writer of Hebrews makes clear that those sacrifices were really just shadows of the ultimate reality of Christ's sacrifice for our sins:

For since the law has but a shadow of the good things to come instead of the true form of these realities, it can never, by the same sacrifices that are continually offered every year, make perfect those who draw near. Otherwise, would they not have ceased to be offered, since the worshipers, having once been cleansed, would no longer have any consciousness of sins? But in these sacrifices there is a reminder of sins every year. For it is impossible for the blood of bulls and goats to take away sins.

Consequently, when Christ came into the world, he said, "Sacrifices and offerings you have not desired, but a body have you prepared for me; in burnt offerings and sin offerings you have taken no pleasure. Then I said, 'Behold, I have come to do your will, O God, as it is written of me in the scroll of the book.'" When he said above, "You have neither desired nor taken pleasure in sacrifices and offerings and burnt offerings and sin offerings" (these are offered according to the law), then he added, "Behold, I have come to do your will." He does away with the first in order to establish the second. And by that will we have been sanctified through the offering of the body of Jesus Christ once for all.

And every priest stands daily at his service, offering repeatedly the same sacrifices, which can never take away sins. But when Christ had offered for all time a single sacrifice for sins, he sat down at the right hand of God, waiting from that time until his enemies should be made a footstool for his feet. For by a single offering he has perfected for all time those who are being sanctified.

Hebrews 10:1-14

What about you? Will you accept Jesus' sacrifice for your sins?

For Further Reflection

Romans 5:6-21: Christ died for the ungodly.

Isaiah 53:1-12: An Old-Testament prophecy about Jesus.

Matthew 26:47-27:54: The trial and crucifixion of Jesus.
(Also Mark 14:43-15:39; Luke 22:47-23:49; John 18:1-19:37)

Book Reference: "The Power of the Blood of Jesus" by Andrew Murray; available free on the internet.

****

Chapter 5
He Has Risen

But the angel said to the women, "Do not be afraid, for I know that you seek Jesus who was crucified. He is not here, for he has risen, as he said." Matthew 28:5-6

For I delivered to you as of first importance what I also received: that Christ died for our sins in accordance with the Scriptures, that he was buried, that he was raised on the third day in accordance with the Scriptures... 1Corinth. 15:3-4

And if Christ has not been raised, your faith is futile and you are still in your sins. 1Corinthians 15:17

The resurrection of Jesus is central to the New Testament, and it is central to our faith. If Jesus has not been raised from the dead, then there is no reason to follow Jesus, there is no reason to consider him to be even a great teacher. The whole New Testament would be one big lie, if Jesus had not physically risen from the dead. All of his original followers would be found to be false witnesses, who foolishly gave their lives for something they knew was a lie.

Jesus himself repeatedly taught that he would die and be raised from the dead. For example:

> *From that time Jesus began to show his disciples that he must go to Jerusalem and suffer many things from the elders and chief priests and scribes, and be killed, and on the third day be raised.* Matthew 16:21

> *"The Son of Man must suffer many things and be rejected by the elders and chief priests and scribes, and be killed, and on the third day be raised."* Luke 9:22

Throughout the book of Acts, Jesus' followers made his resurrection central to their message. For example:

"This Jesus God raised up, and of that we all are witnesses." Acts 2:32

"And we are witnesses of all that he did both in the country of the Jews and in Jerusalem. They put him to death by hanging him on a tree, but God raised him on the third day and made him to appear..." Acts 10:39-40

And Paul went in, as was his custom, and on three Sabbath days he reasoned with them from the Scriptures, explaining and proving that it was necessary for the Christ to suffer and to rise from the dead, and saying, "This Jesus, whom I proclaim to you, is the Christ." Acts 17:2-3

Difficulty in believing in the resurrection of Jesus often arises from one of two roots:

1. Questioning the existence and/or power of God.
2. Questioning whether Jesus actually died.

If the first applies to you, I recommend that you go back to chapter 1 and reconsider the reality of God, and see chapter 9 about God's power. If the second applies, go back to chapter 4 and reconsider the necessity and reality of Jesus' death.

Christ is risen!! Can you respond **"He is risen indeed!!"**?

For Further Reflection

Luke 24:1-53: The resurrection of Jesus.
(Also Matthew 28:1-20, Mark 16:1-20, John 20:1-31)

Acts 2:22-32: Part of Peter's first sermon.

1Corinthians 15:12-21: The importance of the resurrection.

Romans 6:1-14: Implications of the resurrection.

Book Reference: "The Case for Christ" by Lee Strobel.
(Especially Part 3 "Researching the Resurrection")

****

Chapter 6
For God so Loved the World

"For God so loved the world, that he gave his only Son, that whoever believes in him should not perish but have eternal life. For God did not send his Son into the world to condemn the world, but in order that the world might be saved through him." John 3:16-17

"Oh give thanks to the LORD, for he is good, for his steadfast love endures forever!"
1Chronicles 16:34; Psalm 106:1, 107:1, 118:1, 118:29 136:1

Why did God send his Son into the world to die on a cross for our sins? Because *"God so loved the world…"*

Did God send Jesus to die just for people that were already basically good? No, Jesus died to save sinners:

For one will scarcely die for a righteous person— though perhaps for a good person one would dare even to die—but God shows his love for us in that while we were still sinners, Christ died for us. Romans 5:7-8

But God, being rich in mercy, because of the great love with which he loved us, even when we were dead in our trespasses, made us alive together with Christ—by grace you have been saved… Ephesians 2:4-5

But doesn't God delight in sending sinners to hell? No:

"Have I any pleasure in the death of the wicked, declares the Lord GOD, and not rather that he should turn from his way and live?" Ezekiel 18:23

What is God's love like? God's love is like the love a good father has for his children:

How great is the love the Father has lavished on us, that we should be called children of God! And that is what we are! 1John 3:1 NIV

As a father shows compassion to his children, so the LORD shows compassion to those who fear him.

Psalm 103:13

God also likens his love for his people as being stronger than a mother's love for her child:

But Zion said, "The LORD has forsaken me; my Lord has forgotten me."
"Can a woman forget her nursing child, that she should have no compassion on the son of her womb? Even these may forget, yet I will not forget you."

Isaiah 49:14-15

God also likens himself to a bridegroom with his people being his bride:

"Go and proclaim in the hearing of Jerusalem, Thus says the LORD, 'I remember the devotion of your youth, your love as a bride, how you followed me in the wilderness, in a land not sown.'"

Jeremiah 2:2

...as the bridegroom rejoices over the bride, so shall your God rejoice over you.

Isaiah 62:5

Scripture goes so far as to say God *is* love:

So we have come to know and to believe the love that God has for us. God is love, and whoever abides in love abides in God, and God abides in him.

1John 4:16

For Further Reflection

Exodus 34:6-7: Abounding in steadfast love.

Psalm 103:8: Abounding in love.

Psalm 136: His steadfast love endures forever.

Luke 15:11-32: The loving father and prodigal son.

2Peter 3:9: Not wanting any to perish.

Book Reference: "The Way to God" by D.L. Moody. Available free on the internet.

****

Chapter 7
The LORD* Is Good

For the LORD is good; his steadfast love endures forever,
and his faithfulness to all generations.
Psalm 100:5

Oh give thanks to the LORD, for he is good,
for his steadfast love endures forever!
1Chronicles 16:34; Psalm 106:1, 107:1, 118:1, 118:29 136:1

You are good and do good; teach me your statutes.
Psalm 119:68

When the serpent tempted Eve, in Genesis 3, he caused Eve to question God's character. He suggested that God had lied to her, and didn't really want the best for her (Genesis 3:1-5). The same issue faces all of us today. Is God truly good? Can we trust him completely in every area of life?

Eve concluded that the serpent was right, that God did not have her best interests in mind, that God's instructions were not good. So, she chose to disobey God. What about you? Have you bought into the serpent's lie? Do you believe that, at some level, in some way, God is not good?

In speaking of God being "good," I am intending the word "good" in its broadest sense, including every positive attribute that could be used to describe God. Consider the following verses:

The LORD is merciful and gracious, slow to anger and abounding in steadfast love. Psalm 103:8

"For God so loved the world, that he gave his only Son, that whoever believes in him should not perish but have eternal life." John 3:16

The LORD is good to all, and his mercy is over all that he has made. Psalm 145:9

...not wishing that any should perish, but that all should reach repentance. 2Peter 3:9

The LORD is righteous in all his ways and kind in all his works. Psalm 145:17

Gracious is the LORD, and righteous; our God is merciful. Psalm 116:5

...the Lord is compassionate and merciful. James 5:11b

...we have our hope set on the living God, who is the Savior of all people, especially of those who believe. 1Timothy 4:10

God is good; all the time; in every way!

For Further Reflection

Have you ever chosen to disobey God because you thought his ways were not good? How did that work out for you?

Exodus 34:6-7: Merciful and gracious, slow to anger.

Psalm 34: Taste and see that the LORD is good.

Psalm 107: The goodness of God.

Matthew 5:44-45: He sends rain on the just and unjust.

Ephesians 1:3-14: Every spiritual blessing from God.

1Timothy 2:1-4: God desires all people to be saved.

Revelation 21 and 22: A new heaven and a new earth; no more death, or mourning, or crying or pain.

****

* Note: In many Bible translations, the title "the LORD" represents God's personal name ("LORD" with all capital letters; in the Old Testament). There is some uncertainty about the proper pronunciation of God's name, partly due to a tradition that God's name should not be spoken. As a result of this uncertainty and tradition, many translations translate God's name as "the LORD." Some English translations translate God's name more literally as "Yahweh" or "Jehovah."

Chapter 8
The LORD Is Righteous and Just

Righteousness and justice are the foundation of your throne; steadfast love and faithfulness go before you.
Psalm 89:14

But the LORD of hosts is exalted in justice, and the Holy God shows himself holy in righteousness.
Isaiah 5:16

It is unthinkable that God would do wrong, that the Almighty would pervert justice.
Job 34:12 NIV

God is righteous and just. God has never done wrong. God has never wrongly judged anyone.

In Ezekiel's time, however, some of the people accused God of **not** being just:

> *"Yet you say, 'The way of the Lord is not just.'*
> *Hear now, O house of Israel: Is my way not just?*
> *Is it not your ways that are not just?"*   Ezekiel 18:25

The same happens today: People accuse God of not being just, but the reality is that God's accusers are not just. People try to justify their sin by accusing God of having wrong standards. The reality is that they reject true righteousness and justice.

God was righteous and just when he destroyed the world with a flood (Genesis 6 to 8). God was righteous and just when he rained sulfur and fire on Sodom and Gomorrah (Genesis 19). God was righteous and just when he commanded that the Canaanites be destroyed because of their sins (Leviticus 18:24-30; Deuteronomy 9:4-5, 12:29-31, 18:9-12). God was righteous and just when he brought the Babylonian army against his own chosen people (2Chronicles 36:11-21). God is righteous and just whenever he judges people for their sins.

God would be righteous and just to condemn each of us for our sins; *for all have sinned* (Romans 3:23), and *the wages of sin is death* (Romans 6:23).

However, God has no pleasure in the death of the wicked (Ezekiel 18:23). God is not only righteous and just; he is also *merciful and gracious, slow to anger, and abounding in steadfast love* (Exodus 34:6-7). **Righteousness** and **justice** and **love** are all important characteristics of God:

> *The LORD loves righteousness and justice; the earth is full of his unfailing love.*　　　　　Psalm 33:5 NIV

> *"...but let him who boasts boast in this, that he understands and knows me, that I am the LORD who practices steadfast love, justice, and righteousness in the earth. For in these things I delight, declares the LORD."*
> Jeremiah 9:24

It is because of God's righteousness, justice, and love that Jesus went to the cross to redeem us from our sins, so that we would not be condemned. Jesus' sacrifice on the cross is God's perfect provision for our sin, satisfying God's righteous judgment against us through God's love.

> *For the wages of sin is death, but the free gift of God is eternal life in Christ Jesus our Lord.*　　　　Romans 6:23

For Further Reflection

Matthew 5:17-48: God's righteous standards.

Romans 5:6-21: Reconciled to God through Jesus.

Psalm 96:10-13, 98:8-9: God will judge with righteousness.

Matthew 25:31-46: The sheep and the goats.

2Peter 2:1-22: God's judgment on the ungodly.

Revelation 20:11-15: Final judgment.

Isaiah 9:6-7: Justice and righteousness forever.

****

Chapter 9
The LORD Is Great

For I know that the LORD is great,
and that our Lord is above all gods.
Psalm 135:5

Great is the LORD, and greatly to be praised,
and his greatness is unsearchable.
Psalm 145:3

We have seen that God is good, and we have seen that God is righteous and just. But is God *great*? His goodness and righteousness need to be backed up by power to be of value to us. God must be **GREAT** if we are to truly trust in Him. Is God really able to protect us? Is God really able to meet all of our needs? Is God really able to save us in the end? **Is God truly great?**

Consider God's military power:

> *And that night the angel of the LORD went out and struck down 185,000 in the camp of the Assyrians. And when people arose early in the morning, behold, these were all dead bodies.* 2Kings 19:35

> *"Do you think that I cannot appeal to my Father, and he will at once send me more than twelve legions of angels?"* Matthew 26:53

Consider God's power over creation. In His response to Job, God contrasts his own abilities with Job's abilities:

> *"Can you bind the chains of the Pleiades or loose the cords of Orion? Can you lead forth the Mazzaroth in their season, or can you guide the Bear with its children? Do you know the ordinances of the heavens? Can you establish their rule on the earth? Can you lift up your voice to the clouds, that a flood of waters may cover you? Can you send forth lightnings, that they may*

go and say to you, 'Here we are'? Who has put wisdom in the inward parts or given understanding to the mind?" Job 38:31-36

Consider God's wealth:

"Whatever is under the whole heaven is mine."
Job 41:11b

Consider God's knowledge:

Nothing in all creation is hidden from God's sight. Everything is uncovered and laid bare before the eyes of him to whom we must give account. Hebrews 4:13 NIV

Consider God's creative ability:

"Ah, Lord GOD! It is you who have made the heavens and the earth by your great power and by your outstretched arm! Nothing is too hard for you."
Jeremiah 32:17

Consider God's authority:

For the LORD, the Most High, is to be feared, a great king over all the earth. Psalm 47:2

Consider any other attribute by which greatness can be judged, and I think you will agree:

*Great is the LORD, and greatly to be praised,
and his greatness is unsearchable.*
Psalm 145:3

For Further Reflection

Genesis 1: God speaks the heavens and Earth into existence.

Matthew 8:23-27: Jesus calms the storm.

Acts 12:1-24: Peter delivered from prison; James martyred.

Job 38 & 39: More of God's response to Job.

Jeremiah 32:17-19: Nothing too hard.

****

Chapter 10
The LORD Is My Shepherd

The LORD is my shepherd; I shall not want.

He makes me lie down in green pastures.
He leads me beside still waters. He restores my soul.

He leads me in paths of righteousness for his name's sake.

Even though I walk through the valley of the shadow of death,
I will fear no evil, for you are with me;
your rod and your staff, they comfort me.

You prepare a table before me in the presence of my enemies;
you anoint my head with oil; my cup overflows.

Surely goodness and mercy shall follow me all the days of my
life, and I shall dwell in the house of the LORD forever.
Psalm 23:1-6

God cares for his people, for those who truly follow him. Scripture is full of examples of how God provides for his people. Consider a few verses:

> *Oh, fear the LORD, you his saints, for those who fear him have no lack! The young lions suffer want and hunger; but those who seek the LORD lack no good thing.*   Psalm 34:9-10

> *I have been young, and now am old, yet I have not seen the righteous forsaken or his children begging for bread.*   Psalm 37:25

> *For the LORD God is a sun and shield; the LORD bestows favor and honor. No good thing does he withhold from those who walk uprightly.*   Psalm 84:11

> *"For the eyes of the Lord are on the righteous, and his ears are open to their prayer. But the face of the Lord is against those who do evil."*   1Peter 3:12

Did you notice how all those statements were conditional?

They apply to those who *"fear him," "who seek the LORD,"* who are *"righteous," "who walk uprightly."* I am not aware of any scriptures that indicate that God will provide for all the needs of those who don't truly follow him.

Some might rightly inquire: What is included in *"no good thing does he withhold"*? It is human nature to think first that this applies to worldly wealth. However, consider the following verses:

> *Better is the little that the righteous has than the abundance of many wicked. For the arms of the wicked shall be broken, but the LORD upholds the righteous.*
> Psalm 37:16-17

> *Better is a little with the fear of the LORD than great treasure and trouble with it.* Proverbs 15:16

> *Better is a little with righteousness than great revenues with injustice.* Proverbs 16:8

> *How much better to get wisdom than gold! To get understanding is to be chosen rather than silver.*
> Proverbs 16:16

> *Better is a dry morsel with quiet than a house full of feasting with strife.* Proverbs 17:1

> *"Give us this day our daily bread."* Matthew 6:11

From God's perspective, it seems that *"good things"* tend to have spiritual value more than material value. God appears to be first concerned with our spiritual well-being, rather than our physical comfort or worldly success.

For Further Reflection

Do you value material wealth more than spiritual wealth?

Matthew 6:25-34: Don't worry, seek first his kingdom.

Ephesians 1:3-14: Every spiritual blessing in Christ.

1Timothy 6:6-10: Godliness with contentment.

****

Chapter 11
Jesus

On his robe and on his thigh he has a name written,
King of kings and Lord of lords.
Revelation 19:16

This book is written primarily for followers of Jesus. Jesus is central to our faith. In chapter 2 we looked at some of the more-important scriptures about who Jesus is, showing that he is *the Christ*, *the Son of God*, and *Lord of all*. He was *"in the form of God"* before his life on earth, and *"by him all things were created"*!

It is important that we have a clear understanding of Jesus, so that we will not be deceived. Jesus himself warned us:

"See that no one leads you astray. For many will come in my name, saying, 'I am the Christ,' and they will lead many astray."   Matthew 24:4-5

Let's look at some more key points about Jesus. Much of the following list is adapted from some of the "creeds" of early believers.

- **Jesus is the Christ, the Son of God, Lord of all.**
  (chapter 2; Matthew 16:13-17; Mark 1:1, 8:27-30; Luke 1:35; John 11:25-27, 20:26-31; 1John 5:5, Acts 10:36; Romans 10:8-13; 1Corinthians 12:3; Revelation 17:14, 19:11-16)

- **All things were made through him.**
  (John 1:3, 1:10; 1Corinth. 8:6; Colossians 1:15-16; Hebrews 1:1-2)

- **He was conceived by the Holy Spirit.**
  (Matthew 1:18-25; Luke 1:30-35; Philippians 2:5-8)

- **He was born of the virgin Mary.**
  (Isaiah 7:14; Matthew 1:18-25; Luke 1:30-35, 2:1-7)

- **He performed many miracles.**
  (throughout Matthew, Mark, Luke, and John)

- **He suffered under Pontius Pilate.**
  (Matthew 27:11-31; Mark 15:1-20; Luke 23:1-25; John 18:28-19:16)

- **He was crucified, he died, and was buried.**
  (chapter 4; Matthew 27:32-61; Mark 15:21-47; Luke 23:26-56; John 19:17-42; 1Corinthians 15:3-4)

- **He rose from the dead on the third day.**
  (chapter 5; Matthew 28:1-10; Mark 16:1-14; Luke 24:1-12; John 20:1-23; 1Corinthians 15:3-4)

- **He ascended into heaven.**
  (Mark 16:19; Luke 24:50-53; Acts 1:1-11)

- **He is exalted at the right hand of God.**
  (Mark 16:19; Luke 22:69; Acts 2:33, 5:31, 7:55-56; Romans 8:34; Colossians 3:1; Hebrews 1:3, 8:1, 10:12, 12:2)

- **He will come again with glory.**
  (Matthew 16:27; 24:30, 25:31, 26:64; Mark 8:38, 13:26, 14:62; Luke 9:26, 21:27; Acts 1:11; 2Thes. 2:1-8; Rev. 3:11, 22:7, 22:12, 22:20)

- **He will judge the living and the dead.**
  (chapter 14; Matthew 25:31-46; John 5:21-30; Acts 17:29-31; Romans 2:16; 2Timothy 4:1-2; Revelation 20:11-15)

- **His kingdom will have no end.**
  (Isaiah 9:6-7; Daniel 7:13-14; Luke 1:31-33; Hebrews 1:8; Revelation 5:13, 11:15, 22:3-5)

We should especially note that when Jesus comes again it will be obvious to all. As Jesus himself clarified:

> *"So, if they say to you, 'Look, he is in the wilderness,' do not go out. If they say, 'Look, he is in the inner rooms,' do not believe it. For as the lightning comes from the east and shines as far as the west, so will be the coming of the Son of Man."*   Matthew 24:26-27

For Further Reflection

Look up some of the referenced verses to better understand each point, and to verify whether or not scripture actually supports each of the above points.

Read one or more accounts of Jesus' life (in the Bible: Matthew, Mark, Luke, or John).

****

Chapter 12
Your Adversary the Devil

Be sober-minded; be watchful. Your adversary the devil prowls around like a roaring lion, seeking someone to devour. Resist him, firm in your faith, knowing that the same kinds of suffering are being experienced by your brotherhood throughout the world.   1Peter 5:8-9

Put on the whole armor of God, that you may be able to stand against the schemes of the devil. For we do not wrestle against flesh and blood, but against the rulers, against the authorities, against the cosmic powers over this present darkness, against the spiritual forces of evil in the heavenly places.   Ephesians 6:11-12

Scripture clearly portrays that a spiritual realm exists, with both good and bad spiritual beings in it. The devil, or Satan, is portrayed as the leader of the bad. Let's consider further what scripture says about the devil.

The devil is apparently a fallen "cherub" (a type of angel), which God had created. This is understood from Ezekiel 28:12-19, where God speaks of the *"King of Tyre"* as one who formerly was *"on the holy mountain of God"* and in *"Eden, the garden of God."* Further, God says:

> *"Your heart was proud because of your beauty; you corrupted your wisdom for the sake of your splendor. I cast you to the ground; I exposed you before kings, to feast their eyes on you."*   Ezekiel 28:17

The devil hates God, and he hates God's people. Since he can't hurt God directly (since God is great, and the devil is not), he seeks to destroy God's people instead. This is understood from verses such as:

> *Then the dragon became furious with the woman and went off to make war on the rest of her offspring, on*

those who keep the commandments of God and hold to the testimony of Jesus.   Revelation 12:17

Satan's ability to harm God's people is, at least sometimes, limited by God himself, as illustrated in the book of Job:

Then Satan answered the LORD and said, "Does Job fear God for no reason? Have you not put a hedge around him and his house and all that he has, on every side?"   Job 1:9-10

Ephesians 6:10-18 appears to put at least some of the responsibility for overcoming the devil on God's people:

Put on the whole armor of God, that you may be able to stand against the schemes of the devil.   Ephesians 6:11

God provides the spiritual armor, but it is up to us to put it on and stand firm in it. The image given is that of standing firm and defending against an attack; rather than attacking. (Chapter 53 *"Stand Firm"* discusses Ephesians 6:10-18 in more detail.)

The devil will *"flee from you"* if you satisfy the dual conditions of James 4:17:

Submit yourselves therefore to God.   Resist the devil, and he will flee from you.   James 4:7

Without submission to God, it is unlikely that just resisting the devil will cause him to flee.

The nature of the devil is primarily that of a murderer and a liar, as indicated by Jesus:

"You are of your father the devil, and your will is to do your father's desires.   He was a murderer from the beginning, and has nothing to do with the truth, because there is no truth in him.   When he lies, he speaks out of his own character, for he is a liar and the father of lies."   John 8:44

Many scriptures also refer to evil spirits, or "demons." Evil spirits are understood by many to also be fallen angels, but having less power than Satan. Scripture is clear on the existence of demons, but is not so clear regarding their origin, their nature, and how they are able to influence people. (Revelation 12:4 is often referenced to support the belief that a third of the angels rebelled against God with Satan, and became demons on earth.)

Throughout the gospels, demons are observed to live in people, and cause various problems to people so afflicted. Jesus and his disciples had authority over demons and drove them out of people (see scripture references under "For Further Reflection").

In parts of the world that have many followers of Jesus, **experience** suggests that demons have become very secretive, so as to avoid direct confrontation with followers of Jesus, who have authority over them. In other parts of the world, with few followers of Jesus, their activities appear to be generally more open.

In all cases, deception and lies appear to be the primary ways demons influence people, the same as the devil himself. In dealing with demons, followers of Jesus should be careful to not believe the various lies that demons promote, as they are master deceivers, and deception is the main source of their power over people. Simple promotion of truth is generally an effective weapon against them: Expose their lies; trust in Jesus; submit to God and resist them (James 4:7).

Those who are apparently troubled by demons should give particular attention to the issue of forgiveness, as failure to forgive the sins of others appears to give demons access, as implied by Matthew 18:21-35 (see also chapter 22 *"Forgive ..."*). Likewise, unresolved anger may give the devil advantage, as suggested by Ephesians 4:26-27.

If a demon is driven out without proper application of truth to a person's life, the end result may be worse, in accordance with Matthew 12:43-45 and Luke 11:24-26.

Followers of Jesus tend to make one of two mistakes regarding the devil and demons:

1. Ignore them or deny their existence.
2. Attribute too much power and importance to them.

While followers of Jesus should be cautious regarding the devil and demons, there is no reason to fear them, for we have victory over them through Jesus. As scripture says:

> **For I am convinced that neither death nor life, neither angels nor demons, neither the present nor the future, nor any powers, neither height nor depth, nor anything else in all creation, will be able to separate us from the love of God that is in Christ Jesus our Lord.**
>
> Romans 8:38-39 NIV

For Further Reflection

Genesis 3:1-15: The temptation in the garden of Eden. The "serpent" is widely understood to be the devil.

Matthew 4:1-11: The devil tempts Jesus; Jesus uses scripture to resist the temptation. (See also Luke 4:1-13).

Ephesians 6:10-18: Put on the whole armor of God.

Isaiah 14:3-20: A prophecy about the "king of Babylon," understood by many to be referring to the devil.

Ezekiel 28:12-19: Some history about the "king of Tyre," understood by many to be referring to the devil.

Job 1:1 to 2:10: Satan's part in Job's affliction.

Revelation 20:7-10: The devil's end.

Demons cast out: Matthew 8:16, 8:28-34, 9:32-34, 12:22-30, 15:22-28, 17:14-21; Mark 1:23-28, 1:32-34, 1:39, 5:1-20, 6:13, 7:24-30, 9:14-29, 9:38-40; Luke 4:33-37, 6:17-19, 7:21, 8:1-3, 8:26-39, 9:37-42, 11:14-26; Acts 5:16, 8:7-8, 16:16-19, 19:11-17.

Book Reference: "The Bondage Breaker" by Neil Anderson.

Book Reference: "War on the Saints" by Jessie Penn-Lewis and Evan Roberts (1912); the unabridged version is available free on the internet. Somewhat controversial, this book is a thorough look at the activities of the devil and evil spirits.

****

Chapter 13
The Resurrection of the Dead

"And many of those who sleep in the dust of the earth shall awake, some to everlasting life, and some to shame and everlasting contempt. And those who are wise shall shine like the brightness of the sky above; and those who turn many to righteousness, like the stars forever and ever."

Daniel 12:2-3

The priests and the captain of the temple guard and the Sadducees came up to Peter and John while they were speaking to the people. They were greatly disturbed because the apostles were teaching the people and proclaiming in Jesus the resurrection of the dead. Acts 4:1-2 NIV

"...having a hope in God, which these men themselves accept, that there will be a resurrection of both the just and the unjust." Acts 24:15

What do I gain if, humanly speaking, I fought with beasts at Ephesus? If the dead are not raised, "Let us eat and drink, for tomorrow we die." 1Corinthians 15:32

Is there life after death? The above verses clearly show that the answer to this question is YES: *There will be a resurrection of both the just and the unjust.*

If there is no life after death, then nothing really matters much: *"Let us eat and drink, for tomorrow we die."* (1Cor. 15:32). Understanding that there is life after death gives significance to our lives. Our decisions and actions here on earth can have eternal consequences, for good or for bad.

It is somewhat surprising that many of the religious leaders during Jesus' time on Earth (the Sadducees) did not believe in life after death. They tried to find fault with Jesus regarding this issue, reasoning that problems associated with marriage relationships proved their viewpoint against life after death. Jesus replied to them:

"Is this not the reason you are wrong, because you know neither the Scriptures nor the power of God? For when they rise from the dead, they neither marry nor are given in marriage, but are like angels in heaven. And as for the dead being raised, have you not read in the book of Moses, in the passage about the bush, how God spoke to him, saying, 'I am the God of Abraham, and the God of Isaac, and the God of Jacob'? He is not God of the dead, but of the living. You are quite wrong."

Mark 12:24-27

We have additional instruction from 1st Corinthians:

But if there is no resurrection of the dead, then not even Christ has been raised. And if Christ has not been raised, then our preaching is in vain and your faith is in vain. We are even found to be misrepresenting God, because we testified about God that he raised Christ, whom he did not raise if it is true that the dead are not raised. For if the dead are not raised, not even Christ has been raised. And if Christ has not been raised, your faith is futile and you are still in your sins. Then those also who have fallen asleep in Christ have perished. If in Christ we have hope in this life only, we are of all people most to be pitied. But in fact Christ has been raised from the dead... 1Corinthians 15:13-20

For Further Reflection

Mark 12:18-27: The Sadducees question Jesus.
(See also Matthew 22:23-33 and Luke 20:27-38)

John 5:28-29: Jesus on the resurrection of the dead.

John 11:20-26: "I am the resurrection..."

1Corinthians 15:12-58: Paul on the resurrection of the dead.

Philippians 3:10-11: Attain the resurrection from the dead.

Revelation 20:4-6: The first resurrection.

****

Chapter 14
The Day of Judgment

"Then the King will say to those on his right, 'Come, you who are blessed by my Father, inherit the kingdom prepared for you from the foundation of the world.'"

Matthew 25:34

"Then he will say to those on his left, 'Depart from me, you cursed, into the eternal fire prepared for the devil and his angels.'" Matthew 25:41

"I tell you, on the day of judgment people will give account for every careless word they speak…" Matthew 12:36

And if anyone's name was not found written in the book of life, he was thrown into the lake of fire. Revelation 20:15

"The one who conquers will have this heritage, and I will be his God and he will be my son. But as for the cowardly, the faithless, the detestable, as for murderers, the sexually immoral, sorcerers, idolaters, and all liars, their portion will be in the lake that burns with fire and sulfur, which is the second death." Revelation 21:7-8

Throughout scripture, we see the theme of God's righteous judgment. Sometimes his judgment is seen clearly in this life, such as with Noah and the flood (Genesis 6-9). Often his judgment is reserved for after this life, such as with the rich man and Lazarus (Luke 16:19-31). We all deserve God's wrath, since we all have sinned (per chapter 3). There will be a day when God *"will render to each one according to his works"* (Romans 2:6).

But there is great news!!! God has set up an amnesty program. Through faith in Jesus, and through his death on the cross, your sins can be forgiven, so you will not be condemned on the day of judgment:

"For God so loved the world, that he gave his only Son, that whoever believes in him should not perish but have eternal life. For God did not send his Son into the world to condemn the world, but in order that the world might be saved through him. Whoever believes in him is not condemned, but whoever does not believe is condemned already, because he has not believed in the name of the only Son of God." John 3:16-18

Do not wait for the day of judgment to try to get right with God. It will be too late:

Behold, now is the favorable time; behold, now is the day of salvation. 2Corinthians 6:2

If you aren't already a follower of Jesus, or aren't sure about your salvation, then see chapter 16 *"What Must I Do to Be Saved?"* You must *believe* in Jesus to escape condemnation:

Whoever believes in him is not condemned, but whoever does not believe is condemned already, because he has not believed in the name of the only Son of God. John 3:18

"And there is salvation in no one else, for there is no other name under heaven given among men by which we must be saved." Acts 4:12

For Further Reflection

Daniel 12:2: Everlasting life or everlasting contempt.

Matthew 25:31-46: The sheep and the goats.

Luke 16:19-31: The rich man and Lazarus.

John 5:21-30: The resurrection of life or judgment.

Romans 2:5-8: The day of wrath.

1Timothy 2:1-4: God wants all people to be saved.

2Peter 2:4-9: If God did not spare angels...

2Peter 3:1-13: The day of the Lord will come.

1John 4:17-18: Confidence on the day of judgment.

Revelation 20:11-15: The final judgment.

****

Chapter 15
Your Reward in Heaven

Whatever you do, work heartily, as for the Lord and not for men, knowing that from the Lord you will receive the inheritance as your reward. You are serving the Lord Christ. Colossians 3:23-24

"Blessed are you when people insult you, persecute you and falsely say all kinds of evil against you because of me. Rejoice and be glad, because great is your reward in heaven, for in the same way they persecuted the prophets who were before you." Matthew 5:11-12 NIV

Do you expect to get a big reward in this life for following Jesus? Or, do you expect the reward to be in the next life? Do you expect the reward in this life to be greater than the cost in this life?

Many people stop following Jesus as soon as the cost outweighs the immediate reward in this life. As Jesus said:

"...when tribulation or persecution arises on account of the word, immediately they fall away." Mark 4:17

The people who *immediately fall away* fail to understand or value the *future reward* that will be given to those who faithfully follow Jesus.

Certainly, there are benefits in this life for following Jesus. However, the emphasis in the New Testament is on future reward:

If in Christ we have hope in this life only, we are of all people most to be pitied. 1Corinthians 15:19

Part of living by faith is understanding that God rewards those who follow him, and understanding that the reward is primarily in the future, more than in this present age. In speaking of people with faith, the author of Hebrews writes:

And without faith it is impossible to please him, for whoever would draw near to God must believe that he exists and that he rewards those who seek him.

Hebrews 11:6

These all died in faith, not having received the things promised, but having seen them and greeted them from afar, and having acknowledged that they were strangers and exiles on the earth.

Hebrews 11:13

By faith Moses, when he was grown up, refused to be called the son of Pharaoh's daughter, choosing rather to be mistreated with the people of God than to enjoy the fleeting pleasures of sin. He considered the reproach of Christ greater wealth than the treasures of Egypt, for he was looking to the reward.

Hebrews 11:24-26

What about you? Are you looking ahead to a future reward? Or are you looking primarily for reward in this life?

For Further Reflection

Matthew 16:27: Future repayment from Jesus.

Luke 6:35: Great reward.

1Corinthians 3:6-15: Building for a reward.

2Corinthians 5:1-10: An eternal house in heaven.

Ephesians 6:8: Receiving back from the Lord.

1Timothy 6:3-19: Keeping worldly wealth in perspective.

1Peter 1:3-9: An inheritance kept in heaven for you.

1Peter 5:10: Present suffering, eternal glory.

Psalm 73: Present inequality; future glory.

Revelation 22:12: The Lord will repay everyone.

Revelation 21:1-7: A new heaven and a new earth.

Revelation 22:3-5: They will reign forever and ever.

****

PART 2
Things We Do

It is important that we make a distinction between things we are to do ourselves (with strength that God provides), and things that God himself does, or has already done. If we don't make such a distinction, then we may strive in our own strength to do what God has already done, and we may fail to walk in the victory that God has already provided for us.

So, Part 2 focuses on things we are primarily responsible for. The next section, Part 3, will focus on things God is primarily responsible for.

The following verses provide a good starting point:

Do not merely listen to the word, and so deceive yourselves. Do what it says.   James 1:22 NIV

"Everyone then who hears these words of mine and does them will be like a wise man who built his house on the rock. And the rain fell, and the floods came, and the winds blew and beat on that house, but it did not fall, because it had been founded on the rock. And everyone who hears these words of mine and does not do them will be like a foolish man who built his house on the sand. And the rain fell, and the floods came, and the winds blew and beat against that house, and it fell, and great was the fall of it."   Matthew 7:24-27

****

Foundations for Eternal Life

Chapter 16
"What Must I Do to Be Saved?"

And the jailer called for lights and rushed in, and trembling with fear he fell down before Paul and Silas. Then he brought them out and said, "Sirs, what must I do to be saved?" And they said, "Believe in the Lord Jesus, and you will be saved, you and your household." And they spoke the word of the Lord to him and to all who were in his house. And he took them the same hour of the night and washed their wounds; and he was baptized at once, he and all his family.   Acts 16:29-33

There is perhaps no question more important than this one:

"What must I do to be saved?"

Many are too busy with life to consider this question. Many go blindly through life avoiding this question. Many are unwilling to consider that they may be lost.

"What must I do to be saved?"
"Believe in the Lord Jesus, and you will be saved..."
from Acts 16:30-31

Just *"believe"*? What does *"believe"* mean?

You believe that God is one; you do well. Even the demons believe—and shudder!   James 2:19

The demons also know that Jesus is the Christ (Luke 4:41), so a saving belief is clearly more than just an intellectual agreement with truth.

How did Paul clarify "belief" and salvation to the jailer when *"they spoke the word of the Lord to him"*? (Acts 16:32). Near the end of Paul's traveling ministry, in the book of Acts, Paul summarizes the message that he preached:

"I did not shrink from declaring to you anything that was profitable, and teaching you in public and from house to house, testifying both to Jews and to Greeks of

repentance toward God and of faith in our Lord Jesus Christ."   Acts 20:20-21

From this we see that saving belief includes:

1. **Repentance toward God.**
2. **Faith in our Lord Jesus.**

Repentance speaks of a change in thinking; a change from unbelief to belief; a change in the direction of your life. Acknowledge that you have sinned, and turn to God for forgiveness of sins and for deliverance from the power of sin. Choose to follow God rather than continuing to follow after sinful desires. The call to repent applies to everyone:

"In the past God overlooked such ignorance, but now he commands all people everywhere to repent."
                                                                          Acts 17:30 NIV

Faith in Jesus involves believing that Jesus is the promised Messiah (the Christ), the only Son of God, Lord of all; that he died for your sins and the sins of the whole world (1John 2:2); that he rose from the dead; and that he will do for us what scripture says he will do if we follow him.

Having *faith in Jesus* is roughly the same as *believing in Jesus*. *"Faith"* and *"believe"* are similar words in the original Greek language of the New Testament. Both involve conviction and trust, not just mental knowledge. Trusting in Jesus leads us to follow Jesus' teachings.

In the Preface we saw that Jesus invites us to *come* to him for salvation. So, salvation (and repentance and faith) involves coming to Jesus, trusting in Jesus, and following Jesus.

Those who genuinely turn to God in repentance and put their faith in Jesus are "born again" spiritually, and receive God's Holy Spirit to give them new life and purpose (John 3:1-21).

Some people appear to come to saving faith and repentance quickly, primarily as a single event. For others, it appears to happen as a series of more minor steps spread out over time.

Don't wait until you are "good enough" to come to God; it will never happen! You will have victory over sin and have new spiritual life only after you turn to God in repentance and have faith in Jesus. There is no other way to be saved.

What about you? Have you turned to God in repentance? Do you have faith in our Lord Jesus? If not, why not do so today? *"Behold, now is the favorable time; behold, now is the day of salvation."* (2Corinthians 6:2). You can come to God for salvation alone by yourself, or in the presence of others. **Here are some guidelines:**

- **Turn to God in repentance.** Ask God for help with this. True repentance will likely involve things like these:

  - Admit to God that you have sinned against him. Be as specific as you feel is appropriate. Be really honest.

  - Admit to God that you need a savior; that you can't save yourself. You can't fix or undo your own sins.

  - Declare to God that you are now choosing to follow him. Acknowledge that you need his help to do so, that you can't do it by your own strength.

  - Renounce all commitments and allegiances you have made that are contrary to following God.

- **Have faith in our Lord Jesus:**

  - Acknowledge that Jesus is the Christ, the only Son of God, Lord of all. Declare that Jesus is now your Lord.

  - Acknowledge that Jesus died for your sins and rose from the dead.

  - Come to Jesus, trust in Jesus, and follow Jesus.

- **Thank God for his mercy and grace in saving you.**

- **Ask God to fill you with his Spirit**, so that you can live a life pleasing to him.

Baptism: As you have opportunity, get baptized by another follower of Jesus (see chapter 17 "Be Baptized").

For Further Reflection

REGARDING REPENTANCE:

Ezekiel 18:30-32: A call for repentance.

Matthew 3:1-2, Mark 1:4, Luke 3:3: Summaries of John the Baptist's teaching.

Matthew 4:17, Mark 1:15: Summaries of Jesus' teaching.

Matthew 11: 20-24: Because they did not repent.

Mark 6:12: A summary of the 12 disciples' preaching.

Luke 13: 1-5: Jesus emphasizing the need for repentance.

Luke 15:1-7: Jesus teaching about the lost sheep.

Luke 15:8-10: Jesus teaching about the lost coin.

Acts 2:38, 3:19, 5:31: Peter on repentance.

Acts 17:29-31, 20:18-21, 26:19-21: Paul on repentance.

Ephesians 4:20-24: How we came to know Christ.

2Peter 3:9: God wants none to perish; wants all to repent.

Revelation 2:5, 2:14-16, 3:1-3, 3:19-20: Jesus' messages to the churches regarding repentance.

Revelation 9:20-21, 16:9-11: Refusal to repent.

REGARDING FAITH IN JESUS:

John 3:16-18: Whoever believes in Jesus.

John 7:37-39: Whoever believes in Jesus.

Romans 1:17, 3:19-31: Righteous by faith.

Galatians 2:15-16: Justified by faith.

Ephesians 2:8-9: Saved by grace through faith.

Philippians 3:8-9: Righteousness from God.

Hebrews 11:1-40: The "Faith Chapter."

James 2:14-26: Faith without deeds.

Book Reference: "The Way to God" by D.L. Moody. Available free on the internet.

****

Chapter 17
Be Baptized

And Peter said to them, "Repent and be baptized every one of you in the name of Jesus Christ for the forgiveness of your sins, and you will receive the gift of the Holy Spirit."

Acts 2:38

So those who received his word were baptized, and there were added that day about three thousand souls. Acts 2:41

"Go therefore and make disciples of all nations, baptizing them in the name of the Father and of the Son and of the Holy Spirit, teaching them to observe all that I have commanded you. And behold, I am with you always, to the end of the age." Matthew 28:19-20

Water baptism is an outward sign of our salvation. It is a testimony to ourselves and to others that we have chosen to follow Jesus.

A simple understanding of water baptism is that it is a ceremonial washing which symbolizes being washed clean of sin. This understanding is supported by verses such as:

An argument developed between some of John's disciples and a certain Jew over the matter of ceremonial washing. They came to John and said to him, "Rabbi, that man who was with you on the other side of the Jordan—the one you testified about—well, he is baptizing, and everyone is going to him."

John 3:25-26 NIV

"And now why do you wait? Rise and be baptized and wash away your sins, calling on his name." Acts 22:16

Water baptism is an outward symbol of the inward washing that occurs with salvation:

...he saved us, not because of works done by us in righteousness, but according to his own mercy, by the

washing of regeneration and renewal of the Holy Spirit... Titus 3:5

Many also understand water baptism to be a symbol of the death of our old self (being buried with Jesus), and of our being raised up in new life (being raised from the dead with Jesus). This understanding is supported by these scriptures:

> *Do you not know that all of us who have been baptized into Christ Jesus were baptized into his death? We were buried therefore with him by baptism into death, in order that, just as Christ was raised from the dead by the glory of the Father, we too might walk in newness of life.* Romans 6:3-4

> *In him also you were circumcised with a circumcision made without hands, by putting off the body of the flesh, by the circumcision of Christ, having been buried with him in baptism, in which you were also raised with him through faith in the powerful working of God, who raised him from the dead.* Colossians 2:11-12

In some cultures, water baptism carries huge significance, sometimes being interpreted by unbelievers as a rejection of their culture and religious beliefs. A follower of Jesus may be rejected by friends and family because of their new faith, especially after being baptized. It is usually preferable for believers to avoid alienating friends and family. However, sometimes being rejected by friends and family is unavoidable, and a new believer must find new spiritual family among God's people. God will help you through this as you continue to trust in him (Mark 10:29-30, Luke 18:29-30).

For Further Reflection

Matthew 3:1-12: John the Baptist (& Mark 1:1-8, Luke 3:1-20)

Matthew 3:13-17: Jesus' baptism (& Mark 1:9-11, Luke 3:21-22)

Romans 6:1-14: Being buried and raised with Christ.

****

Chapter 18
"Do This in Remembrance of Me"

For I received from the Lord what I also delivered to you, that the Lord Jesus on the night when he was betrayed took bread, and when he had given thanks, he broke it, and said, "This is my body which is for you. Do this in remembrance of me." In the same way also he took the cup, after supper, saying, "This cup is the new covenant in my blood. Do this, as often as you drink it, in remembrance of me." For as often as you eat this bread and drink the cup, you proclaim the Lord's death until he comes. 1Corinthians 11:23-26

Jesus himself directed that we should remember his death by breaking bread and sharing the cup. This simple ritual reminds us that the death of Jesus is central to our faith. It is Jesus' death, especially the shedding of his blood, that redeems us, making forgiveness of sins possible, making our salvation possible. The connection with forgiveness is apparent in the book of Matthew:

And he took a cup, and when he had given thanks he gave it to them, saying, "Drink of it, all of you, for this is my blood of the covenant, which is poured out for many for the forgiveness of sins." Matthew 26:27-28

Scripture also says:

In him we have redemption through his blood, the forgiveness of our trespasses, according to the riches of his grace... Ephesians 1:7

The writer of Hebrews reminds us that:

...without the shedding of blood there is no forgiveness of sins. Hebrews 9:22

Some people claim that Jesus did not actually die on the cross, or that it was really someone else that was crucified, not Jesus himself. On the contrary, the death of Jesus is an essential part of our salvation. **Without the death of Jesus there would be no forgiveness of sins; there would be no salvation for anyone.** Breaking bread together and sharing the cup together reminds us that Jesus died for us.

The details of how the bread and cup are shared vary widely among followers of Jesus. The New Testament provides few specific instructions, so there should be freedom among God's people for various practices. A few clarifications, however, may be helpful:

- Jesus refers to the cup as the *"fruit of the vine"* (Matthew 26:29), so it is generally understood that Jesus was sharing grape juice or wine.

- We share the bread and cup *"in remembrance"* of Jesus and his death, not in the sense of repeating his sacrifice, for scripture indicates that Christ was sacrificed once for all:

  He has no need, like those high priests, to offer sacrifices daily, first for his own sins and then for those of the people, since he did this once for all when he offered up himself. Hebrews 7:27

- The statements by Jesus *"This is my body"* and *"This is my blood"* are widely understood to be figurative, that the bread and wine **represent** his body and blood, not that they literally are his body and blood.

Let's remember that Jesus died for us, so that we might live. Let's share the bread and the cup in remembrance of Jesus. Let's *"proclaim the Lord's death until he comes."*

For Further Reflection

Matthew 26:17-30: The Last Supper.
(Also Mark 14:12-26, Luke 22:7-39)

1Corinthians 11:17-34: Paul's instructions.

Matthew 26:47-27:54: The trial and crucifixion of Jesus.
(Also Mark 14:43-15:39; Luke 22:47-23:49; John 18:1-19:37)

****

Chapter 19
Love the Lord Your God

And one of them, a lawyer, asked him a question to test him. "Teacher, which is the great commandment in the Law?" And he said to him, "You shall love the Lord your God with all your heart and with all your soul and with all your mind. This is the great and first commandment. And a second is like it: You shall love your neighbor as yourself. On these two commandments depend all the Law and the Prophets." Matthew 22:35-40

"The kingdom of heaven may be compared to a king who gave a wedding feast for his son..." Matthew 22:2

"Therefore a man shall leave his father and mother and hold fast to his wife, and the two shall become one flesh." This mystery is profound, and I am saying that it refers to Christ and the church. Ephesians 5:31-32

Then I heard what seemed to be the voice of a great multitude, like the roar of many waters and like the sound of mighty peals of thunder, crying out, "Hallelujah! For the Lord our God the Almighty reigns. Let us rejoice and exult and give him the glory, for the marriage of the Lamb has come, and his Bride has made herself ready; it was granted her to clothe herself with fine linen, bright and pure"—for the fine linen is the righteous deeds of the saints. And the angel said to me, "Write this: Blessed are those who are invited to the marriage supper of the Lamb." And he said to me, "These are the true words of God." Revelation 19:6-9

Love God with your whole being. That, briefly stated, is the greatest commandment. Further, the New Testament likens our relationship with God to a great romance: the marriage of Christ (*"the Lamb"*) to God's people. This marriage is not about a physical/sexual union, but rather about a deep spiritual union.

Consider that God has made romance and marriage partly for this purpose: A deep romance and marriage between a man and a woman is a shadow of the deep intimate relationship that God wants with his people.

Just as it is usually the groom-to-be that initiates the relationship with the bride-to-be, so it is that God has initiated a love relationship with us. Our response to God's love for us should be love for God:

> *We love because he first loved us.*   1John 4:19

Further, God has shown us his passionate love for us through Christ:

> *...but God shows his love for us in that while we were still sinners, Christ died for us.*   Romans 5:8

God showed his love for us by sending Christ to die for us, so our sins could be forgiven, so we would not be condemned. It is natural that the forgiveness we receive from God leads us to deeply love God.

Consider the woman *"who was a sinner"* and who came to Jesus, washed his feet with her tears, and anointed his feet with ointment (Luke 7:36-50). Jesus indicated that this woman had great love for him specifically because she knew that her many sins had been forgiven.

The same should be true of all who follow Jesus: We all had a great debt of sin that we could not pay. Through Jesus' death on a cross, the huge debt we owed has been paid in full, through no effort of our own! Deep, passionate love for God should be our natural response.

A failure to love God deeply is likely related to a failure to understand the depth of your own sin, or a failure to receive God's forgiveness (by not turning to God in repentance and having faith in Jesus; see chapter 16 *"What Must I Do to Be*

Saved?").

How do we know whether or not we really love God?

"If you love me, you will keep my commandments."
John 14:15

For this is the love of God, that we keep his commandments.
1John 5:3

These verses indicate that true love for God results in obedience to God. Just as two romantic lovers try to please each other, so our love for God results in our trying to please God. We try to do things his way, rather than just trying to please ourselves or other people.

But let's be careful here. The above verses are not calling us to try to prove our love for God by trying our best to obey God. Rather, they are indicating that if we truly love God then obedience will be the natural result. As Jesus himself taught:

Jesus answered him, "If anyone loves me, he will keep my word, and my Father will love him, and we will come to him and make our home with him. Whoever does not love me does not keep my words. And the word that you hear is not mine but the Father's who sent me."
John 14:23-24

Let's be even more careful here. Romans 7 appears to show the possibility of being in bondage to sin after salvation, especially if we try to live by law rather than by the Spirit. However, it is clear that the freedom discussed in Romans 8 should be the norm for followers of Jesus, not the bondage of Romans 7. We must be careful to not accept sin as a normal part of a life of faith. Deliberate ongoing sin in a person's life brings that person's very salvation into question (Hebrews 10:26-27).

But some will think: "How burdensome it is to try to obey God!"

For this is the love of God, that we keep his command-

ments. And his commandments are not burdensome. For everyone who has been born of God overcomes the world. 1John 5:3-4

May I suggest that, if your relationship with God is what it should be, obedience to God is **not** burdensome. Obeying God should only seem burdensome if you haven't truly been *"born of God,"* or if your relationship with God isn't based on love for God. I would suggest that, for true lovers of God, disobedience to God is burdensome, not obedience (read about Paul's burden of disobedience in Romans 7).

Also, our love for God should grow deeper as we know him better. This may take some time, just as the love of human romantic relationships should grow deeper with time. An increasing desire to obey God is evidence of an increasing love for God.

What about you? Is there evidence of love for God in your life? Do you desire to obey God? Do you obey God? Is your love for God increasing?

For Further Reflection

Luke 7:36-50: The woman who had lived a sinful life.

1John 2:1-6: We know that we have come to know him…

1John 2:15-17: Do not love the world.

1John 4:20-21: Claiming love for God while hating others.

Revelation 2:1-7: A failure to love God at Ephesus.

Isaiah 62:4-5: God rejoices like a bridegroom.

Jeremiah 2:1 to 3:25: Israel's unfaithfulness toward God likened to adultery and prostitution.

Revelation 21:9-27: The bride, the wife of the Lamb.

****

Chapter 20
Love Your Neighbor as Yourself

And one of them, a lawyer, asked him a question to test him. "Teacher, which is the great commandment in the Law?" And he said to him, "You shall love the Lord your God with all your heart and with all your soul and with all your mind. This is the great and first commandment. And a second is like it: You shall love your neighbor as yourself. On these two commandments depend all the Law and the Prophets."
Matthew 22:35-40

"Love your neighbor as yourself." This command is second only to *"love the Lord your God…"* At first glance, these two commands appear to be simple and straight-forward. But, upon further reflection, they are deep and difficult, perhaps beyond anyone's ability to fully comprehend or to fully comply with.

Let's simply look at scripture for clarification. Keep in mind that some verses focus on love between believers, and some verses apply to our relationships with all people:

"Do not seek revenge or bear a grudge against one of your people, but love your neighbor as yourself. I am the LORD."
Leviticus 19:18 NIV

"A new commandment I give to you, that you love one another: just as I have loved you, you also are to love one another. By this all people will know that you are my disciples, if you have love for one another." John 13:34-35

Love is patient and kind; love does not envy or boast; it is not arrogant or rude. It does not insist on its own way; it is not irritable or resentful; it does not rejoice at wrongdoing, but rejoices with the truth. Love bears all things, believes all things, hopes all things, endures all things. Love never ends.
1Corinthians 13:4-8

"You have heard that it was said, 'You shall love your neighbor and hate your enemy.' But I say to you, Love your enemies and pray for those who persecute you, so that you may be sons of your Father who is in heaven. For he makes his sun rise on the evil and on the good, and sends rain on the just and on the unjust. For if you love those who love you, what reward do you have? Do not even the tax collectors do the same?" Matthew 5:43-46

Beloved, let us love one another, for love is from God, and whoever loves has been born of God and knows God. Anyone who does not love does not know God, because God is love. 1John 4:7-8

If anyone says, "I love God," and hates his brother, he is a liar; for he who does not love his brother whom he has seen cannot love God whom he has not seen. And this commandment we have from him: whoever loves God must also love his brother. 1John 4:20-21

We ought always to give thanks to God for you, brothers, as is right, because your faith is growing abundantly, and the love of every one of you for one another is increasing. 2Thessalonians 1:3

What about you? How deeply do you love others? Is your love for others increasing?

For Further Reflection

Mark: 12:28-34: The greatest commandments.

Luke 10:25-37: The good Samaritan.

Romans 13:8-10: The continuing debt to love one another.

1Corinthians 13:1-13: The "Love" chapter.

Galatians 5:13-15: Serve one another.

James 2:8-9: The royal law found in scripture.

1John 3:10-18: How we know the children of God.

****

Chapter 21
Give

"In all things I have shown you that by working hard in this way we must help the weak and remember the words of the Lord Jesus, how he himself said, 'It is more blessed to give than to receive.'" Acts 20:35

By this we know love, that he laid down his life for us, and we ought to lay down our lives for the brothers. But if anyone has the world's goods and sees his brother in need, yet closes his heart against him, how does God's love abide in him? Little children, let us not love in word or talk but in deed and in truth. 1John 3:16-18

"For God so loved the world, that he gave..." John 3:16

Love for others leads us to take action to help those in need. Because of love, we give our time and resources to help those in need. Consider some more verses about giving:

Share with God's people who are in need. Practice hospitality. Romans 12:13 NIV

"Sell your possessions, and give to the needy. Provide yourselves with moneybags that do not grow old, with a treasure in the heavens that does not fail, where no thief approaches and no moth destroys." Luke 12:33

If your enemy is hungry, give him bread to eat, and if he is thirsty, give him water to drink, for you will heap burning coals on his head, and the LORD will reward you. Proverbs 25:21-22

Do not neglect to show hospitality to strangers, for thereby some have entertained angels unawares. Hebrews 13:2

Do not neglect to do good and to share what you have, for such sacrifices are pleasing to God. Hebrews 13:16

"Give to the one who asks you, and do not turn away from the one who wants to borrow from you."

Matthew 5:42 NIV

John answered, "The man with two tunics should share with him who has none, and the one who has food should do the same."

Luke 3:11 NIV

Let the thief no longer steal, but rather let him labor, doing honest work with his own hands, so that he may have something to share with anyone in need.

Ephesians 4:28

Whoever is generous to the poor lends to the LORD, and he will repay him for his deed.

Proverbs 19:17

The wicked borrows but does not pay back, but the righteous is generous and gives.

Psalm 37:21

Scripture puts some limits on our generosity:

For even when we were with you, we gave you this rule: "If a man will not work, he shall not eat."

2Thessalonians 3:10 NIV

Scripture warns us about giving without having love:

If I give away all I have, and if I deliver up my body to be burned, but have not love, I gain nothing.

1Corinthians 13:3

Finally, scripture calls us to be genuine in our giving:

Each one must give as he has decided in his heart, not reluctantly or under compulsion, for God loves a cheerful giver.

2Corinthians 9:7

For Further Reflection

Matthew 6:1-4: Don't be like the hypocrites.

Matthew 20:20-28: Whoever would be great among you…

Luke 10:25-37: Go and do likewise.

1Timothy 5:3-16: Providing for relatives.

****

Chapter 22
Forgive as the Lord Forgave You

Bear with each other and forgive whatever grievances you may have against one another. Forgive as the Lord forgave you.
Colossians 3:13 NIV

"...and forgive us our debts, as we also have forgiven our debtors."
Matthew 6:12

"For if you forgive others their trespasses, your heavenly Father will also forgive you, but if you do not forgive others their trespasses, neither will your Father forgive your trespasses."
Matthew 6:14-15

"And in anger his master delivered him to the jailers, until he should pay all his debt. So also my heavenly Father will do to every one of you, if you do not forgive your brother from your heart."
Matthew 18:34-35

Forgiveness of our sins, by God, is central to our salvation. Forgiveness is made possible by the sacrifice of Jesus. Forgiveness is not something we earn, it is ours by God's grace, through faith in Jesus (per chapter 29 "Forgiveness of Sins").

Those who have been forgiven by God are expected, in turn, to forgive others. This is a huge issue with God, to the point that Jesus taught:

"...but if you do not forgive others their trespasses, neither will your Father forgive your trespasses."
Matthew 6:15

We saw in chapter 20 (*"Love Your Neighbor..."*) that *"Whoever does not love abides in death."* (1John 3:14). Likewise, a person's failure to forgive others appears to be evidence against their salvation. It could be argued that a failure to forgive others is a failure to love others. Unwillingness to forgive others brings one's salvation into question.

This raises the issue: How can I forgive _____ for what _____ (he/she/they) did? (You fill in the blanks.)

Does forgiving others mean that I forget what they did? Does it mean I must trust them again? No, and No. While forgiveness may impact our memory and trust, these are separate issues. Forgiveness doesn't mean ignoring sin. We can forgive someone, and still follow Jesus' teaching about confronting them (Matthew 18:15-17). In matters of law, legal action may still be appropriate, depending on the situation.

Forgiveness is an act of our will. Forgiveness is choosing to let go of bitterness; choosing to not take revenge; choosing to not bring up the matter in spite; choosing to pray that God would have mercy on the one who offended; choosing to allow for the possibility of reconciliation; choosing to give to others the same kind of grace God has given to us.

Forgiveness is not somehow conjuring up a warm feeling toward others. Forgiving others may not make the pain go away; you may still suffer the consequences of the sin of another. Rather, forgiveness is something we choose to do, by an act of our will, by God's grace, because of love.

Just as *"We love because he first loved us"* so we are to *"Forgive as the Lord forgave you."* God gave the example. In love, he sent Jesus so we could be forgiven. In love, we are likewise called to forgive others. Jesus made it possible.

What about you? Do you need to forgive someone? Will you forgive that person? Do not delay anymore.

For Further Reflection

Proverbs 17:9: He who covers over an offense.

Matthew 18:21-35: The parable of the unmerciful servant.

Mark 11:25: If you have anything against anyone.

Acts 7:59-60: Stephen's prayer.

Romans 12:17-21: Do not repay evil for evil.

****

Chapter 23
Worship, Rejoice, and Give Thanks!

Oh come, let us worship and bow down;
let us kneel before the LORD, our Maker!
Psalm 95:6

Rejoice in the Lord always. I will say it again: Rejoice!
Philippians 4:4 NIV

Oh give thanks to the LORD, for he is good,
for his steadfast love endures forever!
1Chronicles 16:34; Psalm 106:1, 107:1, 118:1, 118:29 136:1

What have you been focusing on recently? God's goodness, his love, and his provision for you? Or, have you been focusing on your own trials and difficulties? Have you been thankful to God for saving you, or have you been mostly grumbling and complaining to God? Have you been rejoicing in the Lord, or cursing his creation?

This is the day the LORD has made; let us rejoice and be glad in it. Psalm 118:24

Which do you prefer to be around: people who *rejoice* and are *glad*, or people who grumble and complain? Which do you prefer for yourself: rejoicing and gladness, or grumbling and complaining? God calls us to *rejoice and be glad.*

No matter how bad your circumstances are, if you are a child of God you can thank God for sending Jesus to save you, and you can thank God and rejoice that your trials are temporary!

Consider Jesus' statement to those who are persecuted:

"Blessed are you when others revile you and persecute you and utter all kinds of evil against you falsely on my account. Rejoice and be glad, for your reward is great in heaven, for so they persecuted the prophets who were before you." Matthew 5:11-12

We should all be able to say, along with Peter:

Blessed be the God and Father of our Lord Jesus Christ! According to his great mercy, he has caused us to be born again to a living hope through the resurrection of Jesus Christ from the dead, to an inheritance that is imperishable, undefiled, and unfading, kept in heaven for you, who by God's power are being guarded through faith for a salvation ready to be revealed in the last time. In this you rejoice, though now for a little while, if necessary, you have been grieved by various trials, so that the tested genuineness of your faith—more precious than gold that perishes though it is tested by fire—may be found to result in praise and glory and honor at the revelation of Jesus Christ. Though you have not seen him, you love him. Though you do not now see him, you believe in him and rejoice with joy that is inexpressible and filled with glory, obtaining the outcome of your faith, the salvation of your souls. 1Peter 1:3-9

If you are a follower of Jesus, you have a glorious future. Your trials in this life, no matter how severe, are temporary.

Worshiping, rejoicing, and giving thanks to God are keys to an empowered spiritual life.

What about you? Will you choose each day to worship, rejoice, and give thanks to God?

For Further Reflection

2Chronicles 20:20-24: Praise and singing ahead of victory.

Psalm 145: A Psalm of praise.

Luke 4:5-8: Worship the Lord only.

Acts 16:22-26: Praying and singing in prison.

Colossians 3:16: Psalms, hymns, and spiritual songs.

Numbers 14:1-38: Grumbling against the LORD.

****

Chapter 24
Prayer

And pray in the Spirit on all occasions with all kinds of prayers and requests. With this in mind, be alert and always keep on praying for all the saints. Ephesians 6:18 NIV

Continue steadfastly in prayer, being watchful in it with thanksgiving. Colossians 4:2

Rejoice always, pray without ceasing... 1Thes. 5:16-17

What is prayer? I am not aware of any scriptures that directly answer this question. Yet, there are many examples of prayer in scripture, especially in the Psalms. I will propose a simple definition: Prayer is communication with God.

Who should pray? Scripture exhorts all followers of Jesus to pray (per the three verses above).

When should we pray? *"On all occasions"* (Ephesians 6:18), and *"without ceasing"* (1Thessalonians 5:17).

How should we pray? *"In the Spirit" "with all kinds of prayers and requests"* (per Ephesians 6:18). Just what *"in the Spirit"* means is open to wide interpretation, but I tend to think of *"in the Spirit"* as being opposite to *"in the flesh,"* as discussed in Romans 8:1-17.

Jesus himself gives us more good direction on how to pray:

"And when you pray, you must not be like the hypocrites. For they love to stand and pray in the synagogues and at the street corners, that they may be seen by others. Truly, I say to you, they have received their reward. But when you pray, go into your room and shut the door and pray to your Father who is in secret. And your Father who sees in secret will reward you.

"And when you pray, do not heap up empty phrases

as the Gentiles do, for they think that they will be heard for their many words. Do not be like them, for your Father knows what you need before you ask him."

Jesus goes on to give a sample prayer, often called "the Lord's prayer," which many followers of Jesus use as a liturgical prayer:

"Pray then like this: 'Our Father in heaven, hallowed be your name. Your kingdom come, your will be done, on earth as it is in heaven. Give us this day our daily bread, and forgive us our debts, as we also have forgiven our debtors. And lead us not into temptation, but deliver us from evil.'"

Matthew 6:9-13

Now it should be clear that the kind of continual prayer that scripture calls us to is not continual repetition of the Lord's prayer. Rather, God wants us to dialogue with him about all aspects of life. Scripture gives us a sense of this:

Do not be anxious about anything, but in everything, by prayer and petition, with thanksgiving, present your requests to God. And the peace of God, which transcends all understanding, will guard your hearts and your minds in Christ Jesus.

Philippians 4:6-7 NIV

For Further Reflection

Pray **Psalm 143**, or another Psalm of your choosing.

Consider memorizing Psalm 143, or another Psalm of your choice (allow yourself several weeks or more to learn it).

Luke 18:1-8: The persistent widow.

Ephesians 3:14-21; Philippians 1:9-11; Colossians 1:9-12: Prayers for the churches.

2Thessalonians 3:1-2: Request for prayer.

James 5:13-18: Prayer.

****

Chapter 25
Examine the Scriptures

Now the Bereans were of more noble character than the Thessalonians, for they received the message with great eagerness and examined the Scriptures every day to see if what Paul said was true.   Acts 17:11 NIV

Followers of Jesus generally understand that the books of the Bible are inspired by God. We view the Bible as a reliable source of truth, which points the way to God. We look to the Bible to learn about God and creation, and to learn how to live in a way that pleases God. As scripture says:

All Scripture is breathed out by God and profitable for teaching, for reproof, for correction, and for training in righteousness, that the man of God may be competent, equipped for every good work.   2Timothy 3:16-17

For whatever was written in former days was written for our instruction, that through endurance and through the encouragement of the Scriptures we might have hope.   Romans 15:4

And we have something more sure, the prophetic word, to which you will do well to pay attention as to a lamp shining in a dark place, until the day dawns and the morning star rises in your hearts, knowing this first of all, that no prophecy of Scripture comes from someone's own interpretation. For no prophecy was ever produced by the will of man, but men spoke from God as they were carried along by the Holy Spirit.   2Peter 1:19-21

The Bible is divided into two main sections: the Old Testament and the New Testament. The Old Testament contains 39 "books" written before Jesus' life on earth. The New Testament contains 27 "books" written after Jesus' life on earth. Here is a very brief outline of the Bible:

OLD TESTAMENT BOOKS:

Genesis through Deuteronomy: Five books widely believed to be written by Moses. They record what happened from creation to Moses' death, and include the law of Moses.

Joshua through Esther (12 books): Historical books, covering the time period from Moses' death to the building of the second temple in Jerusalem (roughly 517 BC).

Job: The story of Job's suffering and deliverance.

Psalms: Prayers and songs written by several authors.

Proverbs: About wisdom, mostly written by King Solomon.

Ecclesiastes: More wisdom from King Solomon, showing what life looks like from the perspective of "under the sun."

Song of Solomon: By King Solomon; about romantic love.

Isaiah through Malachi (17 books): The Prophets, calling the people to turn back to God.

NEW TESTAMENT BOOKS:

Matthew, Mark, Luke and John (or "The Gospel according to ..."): Four accounts of Jesus' life. Each book is named for its author.

Acts (or "The Acts of the Apostles"): An account of what happened after Jesus rose from the dead, written by Luke.

Romans through Philemon (13 books): Letters from Paul the apostle, to various churches and individuals. Each book is named for its original recipient.

Hebrews through Jude (8 books): Other letters to God's people. Each book is named for its author, except for Hebrews (the author of Hebrews is uncertain).

Revelation: A revelation from Jesus to John. It includes letters to seven churches, and prophecies about the future.

The books of the Old Testament were mostly written in the Hebrew language, and the books of the New Testament were mostly written in the Greek language. The Bible has been translated into many languages, and most believers read and study a translation in their own language, rather than trying to learn to read Hebrew and Greek.

We should keep in mind that the purpose of the Bible is to show us how to know and follow God. Some people wrongly make knowing the Bible their primary goal, rather than knowing and following God. Be careful not to be like the people Jesus spoke of:

> *"You search the Scriptures because you think that in them you have eternal life; and it is they that bear witness about me, yet you refuse to come to me that you may have life."* John 5:39-40

It is important to understand that much of the Old Testament relates to "the law" given by God through Moses. This "law of Moses" was mostly given in the books of Exodus and Leviticus. The law of Moses made the people aware of sin and required various animal sacrifices for the people to be in right relationship with God. However, the law of Moses could not make the people righteous, or provide a final solution for sin. The law of Moses pointed to the final solution that Jesus would provide. As scripture says:

> *So the law was put in charge to lead us to Christ that we might be justified by faith. Now that faith has come, we are no longer under the supervision of the law.* Galatians 3:24-25 NIV

I personally make a distinction between the "law of Moses" (an imperfect law intended to restrain sin and direct people toward Christ) and the "law of the LORD" (God's perfect eternal moral law, which is praised in the Psalms).

Ask God for wisdom and understanding as you read the Bible. If you are not familiar with the Bible, I recommend that you start by reading about the life of Jesus, in the book of Matthew, Mark, Luke, or John.

Finally, consider the goodness of the word of God:

I have stored up your word in my heart, that I might not sin against you. Psalm 119:11

I will delight in your statutes; I will not forget your word. Psalm 119:16

Your commandment makes me wiser than my enemies, for it is ever with me. I have more understanding than all my teachers, for your testimonies are my meditation. I understand more than the aged, for I keep your precepts. I hold back my feet from every evil way, in order to keep your word. Psalm 119:98-101

How sweet are your words to my taste, sweeter than honey to my mouth! Psalm 119:103

Your word is a lamp to my feet and a light to my path. Psalm 119:105

Your promise is well tried, and your servant loves it. Psalm 119:140

I rejoice at your word like one who finds great spoil. Psalm 119:162

For Further Reflection

Psalm 1: Blessed is the man…

Psalm 19:7-11: More to be desired than gold.

Psalm 119: The goodness of God's word.

Matthew 5:17-48: Jesus clarifies God's perfect law.

Matthew 22:29: You do not know the scriptures.

Hebrews 10:1-14: The law as a shadow.

James 1:22-25: Be doers of the word…

Find at least one verse in the Bible that is meaningful to you, and start memorizing it today.

Bible Software: If you have a compatible computer, tablet, or smart phone, free Bible study software may be available at www.e-sword.net. For Android phones: www.mysword.info. (Bible translations in many languages are available.)

****

Chapter 26
Meeting Together

And let us consider how we may spur one another on toward love and good deeds. Let us not give up meeting together, as some are in the habit of doing, but let us encourage one another—and all the more as you see the Day approaching. Hebrews 10:24-25 NIV

Those who accepted his message were baptized, and about three thousand were added to their number that day. They devoted themselves to the apostles' teaching and to the fellowship, to the breaking of bread and to prayer.
Acts 2:41-42 NIV

Every day they continued to meet together in the temple courts. They broke bread in their homes and ate together with glad and sincere hearts, praising God and enjoying the favor of all the people. And the Lord added to their number daily those who were being saved. Acts 2:46-47 NIV

Acts 2:42 (above) indicates four things the early believers *devoted themselves to*:

- *The apostles' teaching*: They learned together.
- *Fellowship*: They shared life together.
- *The breaking of bread*: They broke bread together.
  (This may refer to having meals together and/or remembering Jesus' death per chapter 18 *"Do This in Remembrance of Me."*)
- *Prayer*: They prayed together.

Hebrews 10:24-25 (above) indicates that a primary purpose of *meeting together* is to *spur one another on toward love and good deeds*, and to *encourage one another.*

Consider some additional verses:

Let the word of Christ dwell in you richly, teaching and admonishing one another in all wisdom, singing psalms and hymns and spiritual songs, with thankfulness in your hearts to God. Colossians 3:16

Therefore encourage one another and build one another up, just as you are doing. 1Thessalonians 5:11

Therefore, confess your sins to one another and pray for one another, that you may be healed. James 5:16

If you don't already have good relationships with other believers, I encourage you to seek to develop such relationships. Everyone's situation is unique, so it is difficult to give specific direction. Ask God for discernment in this area. As you consider various options for *meeting together* with other believers, keep in mind that the spiritual strength of a particular group of believers is often more dependent on the local people involved and local leadership, rather than on a larger organization which they may be part of. Look for leaders who follow Jesus' example:

But Jesus called them to him and said, "You know that the rulers of the Gentiles lord it over them, and their great ones exercise authority over them. It shall not be so among you. But whoever would be great among you must be your servant, and whoever would be first among you must be your slave, even as the Son of Man came not to be served but to serve, and to give his life as a ransom for many." Matthew 20:25-28

For Further Reflection

Do you have strong relationships with other believers?

What should you do to develop or strengthen relationships?

Ecclesiastes 4:9-12: Two are better than one.

Romans 16:17-18: Watch out for those who cause divisions.

1Corinthians 14:26-31: When you come together.

2Corinthians 6:14-18: Believers and unbelievers.

****

Chapter 27
Obey

"If you love me, you will obey what I command."
John 14:15 NIV

And by this we know that we have come to know him, if we keep his commandments. Whoever says "I know him" but does not keep his commandments is a liar, and the truth is not in him, but whoever keeps his word, in him truly the love of God is perfected. By this we may know that we are in him: whoever says he abides in him ought to walk in the same way in which he walked.   1John 2:3-6

As he said these things, a woman in the crowd raised her voice and said to him, "Blessed is the womb that bore you, and the breasts at which you nursed!" But he said, "Blessed rather are those who hear the word of God and keep it!"   Luke 11:27-28

Obedience to God is an important result of our salvation. We are not saved by obedience to God's commands, rather we obey because we are saved. As we saw previously, obedience is a natural result of our love for God:

Jesus answered him, "If anyone loves me, he will keep my word, and my Father will love him, and we will come to him and make our home with him. Whoever does not love me does not keep my words. And the word that you hear is not mine but the Father's who sent me."
John 14:23-24

For this is the love of God, that we keep his commandments.   1John 5:3

We must not follow the example of the teachers of the law and Pharisees. Jesus rebuked them in Matthew 23 because they focused on an outward appearance of righteousness, rather than having true inward righteousness. Don't be deceived; God knows your heart. God wants you to have an inward righteousness that only comes from him:

> **Therefore no one will be declared righteous in his sight by observing the law; rather, through the law we become conscious of sin. But now a righteousness from God, apart from law, has been made known, to which the Law and the Prophets testify. This righteousness from God comes through faith in Jesus Christ to all who believe.**
>
> Romans 3:20-22 NIV

> **...not having a righteousness of my own that comes from the law, but that which is through faith in Christ— the righteousness that comes from God and is by faith.**
>
> Philippians 3:9 NIV

Whether or not we are living like God calls us to live is a measure of our own spiritual health. Consider your own life. How are you doing regarding the last few chapters?

- Do your actions show that you love your neighbor?
- Do you forgive those who sin against you?
- Do you worship, rejoice, and give thanks to God?
- Do you pray on all occasions?
- Do you love God's word? Do you spend time in it?
- Do you have fellowship with other believers?
- Do you desire to obey God in all things?

If you judge yourself to be weak on most of these points, I recommend that you reconsider chapter 16 *"What Must I Do to Be Saved?"* and be sure that you understand God's marvelous grace, which is the subject of the next section.

For Further Reflection

Romans 6:16-23: Slaves of righteousness.

2Corinthians 13:5: Examine yourselves.

Philippians 3:1-16: Righteousness from God.

Hebrews 10:26-31: If we go on sinning deliberately...

****

PART 3
Things God Does

Part 2 focused on things we are called to do. Part 3 focuses on things God does, or things God has already done. More specifically, we'll look at the grace that God gives to all who follow Jesus:

- Because Jesus shed his blood,
            our sins are forgiven.

- Because Jesus died,
            we are set free from sin.

- Because Jesus rose from the dead,
            we have new life.

- Because Jesus is exalted,
            the Holy Spirit is poured out.

- We are members of one body,
            the body of Christ.

- God has given us every spiritual blessing
            in Christ.

            ****

Foundations for Eternal Life

Chapter 28
Grace

And from his fullness we have all received, grace upon grace. For the law was given through Moses; grace and truth came through Jesus Christ. John 1:16-17

For you know the grace of our Lord Jesus Christ, that though he was rich, yet for your sake he became poor, so that you by his poverty might become rich. 2Corinthians 8:9

For the grace of God that brings salvation has appeared to all men. Titus 2:11 NIV

"Amazing grace, how sweet the sound, that saved a wretch like me!" (John Newton). Oh, the wonder of God's grace!!

What is grace? Grace is often defined as "unmerited favor" or "unmerited blessing." "Unmerited" means we don't deserve it; we haven't earned it. God's grace is involved in all of the many blessings God gives us; all of which we don't deserve. When we say that *"God is love"* (1John 4:16) we are speaking of God's character and compassion. When we speak of God's *grace*, we are speaking of God's provision for us: things God gives us, or things God does for us. Grace may be thought of as God's provision for us resulting from his love for us. This is illustrated by this well-known verse:

"For God so loved the world, that he gave his only Son, that whoever believes in him should not perish but have eternal life." John 3:16

God giving *his only Son* is a supreme act of grace. Why did God do that? Because *God so loved the world.*

Salvation is possible only by God's grace:

For by grace you have been saved through faith. And this is not your own doing; it is the gift of God, not a result of works, so that no one may boast. Ephesians 2:8-9

The following six chapters will look at various aspects of God's grace given to those who are saved, to those who turn to God in repentance and have faith in Jesus (per chapter 16):

- Because Jesus shed his blood, our sins are forgiven.
- Because Jesus died, we are set free from sin.
- Because Jesus rose from the dead, we have new life.
- Because Jesus is exalted, the Holy Spirit is poured out.
- We are members of one body, the body of Christ.
- God has given us every spiritual blessing in Christ.

Similarly, the next section is about *"Things God and We Do."* All of the things discussed in those chapters also involve God's grace toward us: faith, hope, love, walking by the Spirit, the fruit of the spirit, different gifts, and laying on of hands. The grace of God can be understood to include every good thing God gives us or does for us. It's not surprising that Paul summarized the ministry that he received from the Lord Jesus as this: *"to testify to the gospel of the grace of God."* (Acts 20:24).

Thank you, God, for your grace that is ours through Jesus!

For Further Reflection

Luke 15:11-32: A father's example of grace.

Romans 5:1-2: Gaining access to grace through faith.

Romans 5:15-21: Abundant grace.

Romans 12:6-8: Gifts that differ according to grace given.

2Corinthians 9:8: God is able to make all grace abound.

Galatians 5:4: Fallen from grace.

Titus 2:11-15: The grace of God teaches us.

Hebrews 4:14-16: Find grace to help in time of need.

Hebrews 12:14-16: Don't fail to obtain the grace of God.

James 4:6, 1Peter 5:5: God gives grace to the humble.

1Peter 4:10-11: Be good stewards of God's grace.

Jude 1:4: Perverting the grace of God.

****

Chapter 29
Forgiveness of Sins

Blessed is he whose transgressions are forgiven, whose sins are covered. Blessed is the man whose sin the LORD does not count against him and in whose spirit is no deceit.

Psalm 32:1-2 NIV

In him we have redemption through his blood, the forgiveness of our trespasses, according to the riches of his grace...

Ephesians 1:7

What a tremendous blessing it is to have our sins forgiven by God! What a marvelous sacrifice Jesus made so that we could be forgiven! How wonderful is God's grace!

Forgiving others when they sin against us is something we are individually responsible for doing (per chapter 22). But us forgiving each other doesn't save us; it is God's forgiveness of us that makes salvation possible. This is something only God can do.

We should keep in mind that forgiveness of our sins is possible only because Jesus shed his blood for us:

> *...without the shedding of blood there is no forgiveness of sins.*
> Hebrews 9:22

> *For it is impossible for the blood of bulls and goats to take away sins.*
> Hebrews 10:4

> *And he took a cup, and when he had given thanks he gave it to them, saying, "Drink of it, all of you, for this is my blood of the covenant, which is poured out for many for the forgiveness of sins."*
> Matthew 26:27-28

It is because of God's grace, because of Jesus shedding his blood, that our sins can be forgiven. There is nothing we can do to earn forgiveness by God. It is something we receive freely from God through faith in Jesus.

While Jesus' sacrifice is sufficient for the forgiveness of all the sins of everyone, it is clear that not everyone's sins are forgiven, or will be forgiven. Forgiveness of sins is a gift from God to those who are saved, to those who turn to God in repentance and have faith in Jesus (per chapter 16). We must each **believe in the Lord Jesus** (Acts 16:31) for our sins to be forgiven, otherwise God's wrath remains on us:

> *"Whoever believes in the Son has eternal life, but whoever rejects the Son will not see life, for God's wrath remains on him."*   John 3:36 NIV

Further, if (or when) we sin after becoming followers of Jesus, we are to confess our sins to God:

> *If we confess our sins, he is faithful and just to forgive us our sins and to cleanse us from all unrighteousness.*
> 1John 1:9

Finally, forgiveness of sins is central to the good news that is to be preached:

> *Then he opened their minds to understand the Scriptures, and said to them, "Thus it is written, that the Christ should suffer and on the third day rise from the dead, and that repentance and forgiveness of sins should be proclaimed in his name to all nations, beginning from Jerusalem."*   Luke 24:45-47

Thank you, God, for forgiving all our sins through Jesus!

For Further Reflection

Matthew 6:14-15: For if you forgive men when they sin…

Mark 2:1-12, Luke 5:17-26: "Who can forgive sins….?"

Acts 10:43: Forgiveness of sins through his name.

Acts 26:15-18: That they may receive forgiveness of sins.

Colossians 1:13-14: For he has rescued us…

****

Chapter 30
Set Free From Sin

We know that our old self was crucified with him in order that the body of sin might be brought to nothing, so that we would no longer be enslaved to sin. For one who has died has been set free from sin. Romans 6:6-7

For the death he died he died to sin, once for all, but the life he lives he lives to God. So you also must consider yourselves dead to sin and alive to God in Christ Jesus. Let not sin therefore reign in your mortal body, to make you obey its passions. Romans 6:10-12

We know that everyone who has been born of God does not keep on sinning, but he who was born of God protects him, and the evil one does not touch him. We know that we are from God, and the whole world lies in the power of the evil one. 1John 5:18-19

Prior to being **born of God**, we were all under **the power of the evil one**; we were **enslaved to sin.** Through repentance and faith (chapter 16) we are **born of God,** and **set free from sin**!

Forgiveness of sin is primarily associated with Jesus' shed blood (per the previous chapter). However, deliverance from the power of sin is primarily associated with Jesus' death and resurrection. We especially focus on the death of Jesus in this chapter, and how being united with Jesus in his death sets us free from sin's power.

Freedom from sin is primarily part of God's grace. Through Jesus, God **has** set his people free from sin's dominion. The power of sin has been broken. However, we must still learn how and choose to live as servants of God rather than servants of sin, as scripture emphasizes in Romans 6:15-23.

Identifying ourselves with Jesus' death and resurrection solves the problem of sin's dominion over us. *We know that our old self was crucified with him* (Romans 6:6). His death is our own death, setting us free from the dominion of sin:

For one who has died has been set free from sin.

Romans 6:7

Paul's letter to the Romans indicates some key points to make freedom from sin's dominion a practical reality:

- We must *know* these things (per Romans 6:6-7 above).

- We must identify ourselves with Jesus' death and resurrection:

  So you also must consider yourselves dead to sin and alive to God in Christ Jesus. Romans 6:11

- We are to present ourselves to God:

  Do not present your members to sin as instruments for unrighteousness, but present yourselves to God as those who have been brought from death to life, and your members to God as instruments for righteousness.

  Romans 6:13

- We are to walk in newness of life:

  We were buried therefore with him by baptism into death, in order that, just as Christ was raised from the dead by the glory of the Father, we too might walk in newness of life. Romans 6:4

(If you need additional help to live free from sin's power, please refer to the books referenced below.)

Thank you, God, for setting us free from sin through Jesus!

For Further Reflection

John 8:34-36: Everyone who practices sin is a slave to sin.

Romans chapters 5 to 8: Sin and righteousness.

Galatians 5:1-4: Christ has set us free.

Colossians 3:1-10: For you have died.

Book Reference: "The Bondage Breaker" by Neil Anderson.

Book Reference: "The Secret of the Cross" by Andrew Murray; a 32-day devotional; available free on the internet.

****

Chapter 31
Born of God

Everyone who believes that Jesus is the Christ has been born of God, and everyone who loves the Father loves whoever has been born of him. 1John 5:1

He came to his own, and his own people did not receive him. But to all who did receive him, who believed in his name, he gave the right to become children of God, who were born, not of blood nor of the will of the flesh nor of the will of man, but of God. John 1:11-13

Praise be to the God and Father of our Lord Jesus Christ! In his great mercy he has given us new birth into a living hope through the resurrection of Jesus Christ from the dead... 1Peter 1:3 NIV

Not only are our sins forgiven through God's grace (per chapter 29), and we are delivered from the power of sin (chapter 30), but we also have new life from God! When we are saved we are **born of God.** This **new birth** is given to us **through the resurrection of Jesus Christ from the dead** (1Peter 1:3). Because Jesus rose from the dead, all who follow him are given new life. The spiritual death we inherited from Adam (chapter 3) is replaced with spiritual life!

The need for new spiritual life in us should be apparent from the dominion of sin in our lives before we are saved:

As for you, you were dead in your transgressions and sins... Ephesians 2:1 NIV

But because of his great love for us, God, who is rich in mercy, made us alive with Christ even when we were dead in transgressions—it is by grace you have been saved. Ephesians 2:4-5 NIV

The absolute need to be **born again** is made clear by Jesus:

"Truly, truly, I say to you, unless one is born again he cannot see the kingdom of God."   John 3:3

The experience of being *"born again"* or *"born of God"* or *"made alive with Christ"* (etc.) varies widely among believers. For some it is a sudden dynamic experience resulting from a definite decision. For others it may appear to be a more gradual process. For everyone the path to being born again includes somehow turning to God (repentance) and somehow developing faith in Jesus (per chapter 16).

Just how *new birth* happens is not very clear in scripture. Jesus compares being *born again* to the wind. We may not understand it, but we are aware that it happens:

"You should not be surprised at my saying, 'You must be born again.' The wind blows wherever it pleases. You hear its sound, but you cannot tell where it comes from or where it is going. So it is with everyone born of the Spirit."   John 3:7-8 NIV

What about you? Have you been *born of God*? If not, or you're not sure, I recommend that you review chapter 16 *"What Must I Do to Be Saved?"*

If you are already *born of God*, then join me in saying: Thank you, God, for making us *alive with Christ*!

For Further Reflection

Romans 5:12-21: Death through Adam; life through Jesus.

Romans 6:13: Brought from death to life.

2Corinthians 5:17: A new creation.

Ephesians 2:1-7: Dead in sin; made alive with Christ.

Titus 3:4-7: The washing of regeneration.

1Peter 1:22-23: You have been born again.

1John 3:9, 4:7, 5:4, 5:18: Born of God.

1John 3:14: Passed from death to life.

1John 5:11-12: He who has the Son has life.

****

Chapter 32
The Gift of the Holy Spirit

John answered them all, saying, "I baptize you with water, but he who is mightier than I is coming, the strap of whose sandals I am not worthy to untie. He will baptize you with the Holy Spirit and with fire."   Luke 3:16

"If anyone thirsts, let him come to me and drink. Whoever believes in me, as the Scripture has said, 'Out of his heart will flow rivers of living water.'" Now this he said about the Spirit, whom those who believed in him were to receive, for as yet the Spirit had not been given, because Jesus was not yet glorified.   John 7:37-39

"Exalted to the right hand of God, he has received from the Father the promised Holy Spirit and has poured out what you now see and hear."   Acts 2:33 NIV

And Peter said to them, "Repent and be baptized every one of you in the name of Jesus Christ for the forgiveness of your sins, and you will receive the gift of the Holy Spirit."   Acts 2:38

What a marvelous gift the Holy Spirit is… the Spirit of God living in us! How marvelous is God's grace!

The gift of the Holy Spirit is for all believers:

> *"For the promise is for you and for your children and for all who are far off, everyone whom the Lord our God calls to himself."*   Acts 2:39

The pouring out of the Holy Spirit is done by Jesus, and is the result of Jesus being *"exalted to the right hand of God"* (per Acts 2:33 above).

In what ways does the Holy Spirit help us?

> *"…the Holy Spirit, whom the Father will send in my name, he will teach you all things and bring to your remembrance all that I have said to you."*   John 14:26

Now we have received not the spirit of the world, but the Spirit who is from God, that we might understand the things freely given us by God. 1Corinthians 2:12

Now the Lord is the Spirit, and where the Spirit of the Lord is, there is freedom. 2Corinthians 3:17

I pray that out of his glorious riches he may strengthen you with power through his Spirit in your inner being... Ephesians 3:16 NIV

From these verses we see that the Holy Spirit teaches us, reminds us, helps our understanding, brings us freedom, and gives us power.

The Holy Spirit also gives special abilities to God's people, as indicated in 1st Corinthians chapter 12. It is important to understand that these abilities or gifts are not all given to all believers, but rather *"he gives them to each one, just as he determines"* (1Corinthians 12:11 NIV). Some people teach that the Holy Spirit gives a particular gift to all true believers, or that some of the gifts are no longer given to anyone. I prefer simply: *"he gives them to each one, just as he determines."* See chapter 40 *"Different Gifts"* for more on this subject.

Thank you, God, for the gift of the Holy Spirit!

For Further Reflection

Luke 11:11-13: Giving the Holy Spirit to those who ask.

John 14:15-18, 14:23-27, 16:7-15: The Helper.

John 20:21-23: "Receive the Holy Spirit."

Acts 2:1-47: The Holy Spirit at Pentecost.

1Corinthians 3:16-17, 6:18-20: You are God's temple.

Eph. 1:13-14: A seal and a deposit. (Also 2Cor. 1:21-22, 5:5)

1John 2:20 & 27: Anointed by the Holy One.

1John 4:1-6: Test the spirits.

Book Reference: "Secret Power" or "The Secret of Success in Christian Life and Work" by D.L. Moody (the same book, two different titles). Available free on the internet.

****

Chapter 33
One Body

Just as each of us has one body with many members, and these members do not all have the same function, so in Christ we who are many form one body, and each member belongs to all the others.   Romans 12:4-5 NIV

Now you are the body of Christ and individually members of it.   1Corinthians 12:27

This mystery is that the Gentiles are fellow heirs, members of the same body, and partakers of the promise in Christ Jesus through the gospel.   Ephesians 3:6

Therefore, having put away falsehood, let each one of you speak the truth with his neighbor, for we are members one of another.   Ephesians 4:25

By God's grace, followers of Jesus are members of the greatest organization on earth: **the body of Christ.**

It is common for us to think that the primary benefits of salvation relate to what God does for us: forgiveness of sin, freedom from sin's power, eternal life, and other blessings that are ours in Christ. We are slower to understand that by following Jesus we each have become part of the world-wide **body of Christ**, and **each member belongs to all the others.**

I like to think of this **one body** teaching this way: We are each part of a huge family, God's family, and we are each responsible to help and encourage one another.

Being members of one body is contrary to normal human divisions. As scripture says:

> *There is neither Jew nor Greek, slave nor free, male nor female, for you are all one in Christ Jesus.*
> Galatians 3:28 NIV

"Neither Jew nor Greek" indicates that cultural and

religious backgrounds should not divide us. *"Slave nor free"* indicates that such things as position and class should not divide us. *"Male nor female"* indicates that gender should not divide us.

Consider some other distinctions that I believe should not divide God's true people: age, wealth or poverty, physical abilities or disabilities, mental abilities or disabilities, education, nationality, school affiliations, social affiliations, church affiliations, and theological differences.

Unfortunately, God's people often appear to be divided by one or more of the above distinctions. Dear Friends, this should not be. Jesus said:

> *"By this all people will know that you are my disciples, if you have love for one another."*   John 13:35

May God give us all discernment to turn away from ungodly divisions, and to love and serve one another as *"one body."*

Thank you, God, for making us, your people, *one body*.

For Further Reflection

John 10:14-16: One flock.

John 17:9-23: So that they may be one.

Romans 12:16: Associate with the lowly.

Romans 16:17-18: Watch out for those who cause divisions.

1Corinthians 10:16-17: One bread, one body.

1Corinthians 12:12-31: One body, many members.

2Corinthians 8:1-15: An offering for God's people.

Ephesians 4:4-6: One body and one Spirit.

Colossians 3:9-11: No Greek or Jew...

James 2:1-9: Show no partiality.

3John 1:5-12: Welcoming the brothers.

****

Chapter 34
Every Spiritual Blessing

Praise be to the God and Father of our Lord Jesus Christ, who has blessed us in the heavenly realms with every spiritual blessing in Christ. Ephesians 1:3 NIV

His divine power has given us everything we need for life and godliness through our knowledge of him who called us by his own glory and goodness. 2Peter 1:3 NIV

God's grace given to those who follow Jesus includes *"every spiritual blessing in Christ."* What are some of these spiritual blessings? We have a list in Ephesians 1:

- *...he chose us in him before the foundation of the world, that we should be holy and blameless before him.*
  Ephesians 1:4

  Before creation, God chose that we, his people, would be *holy and blameless before him.* This righteous state before God is made possible by other spiritual blessings: forgiveness of our sins through Jesus' shed blood, and the washing of rebirth and renewal by the Holy Spirit.

- *In love he predestined us for adoption as sons through Jesus Christ...* Ephesians 1:5

  All who follow Jesus are *predestined* to be adopted as his sons, apparently in the same sense as in Romans 8:23: *"...as we wait eagerly for our adoption as sons, the redemption of our bodies."*

- *In him we have redemption through his blood, the forgiveness of our trespasses...* Ephesians 1:7

  All who follow Jesus have been redeemed! We are no longer lost and condemned; our sins have been forgiven! (as discussed in chapter 29). Jesus shed his blood for me and for you, to give us this spiritual blessing.

- *And he made known to us the mystery of his will…*

Ephesians 1:9 NIV

Much that was hidden during Old-Testament times is now made known. We now understand that God's purpose is *"to bring all things in heaven and on earth together under one head, even Christ."* (Ephesians 1:10 NIV)

- *In him we have obtained an inheritance, having been predestined according to the purpose of him who works all things according to the counsel of his will…*

Ephesians 1:11

We are *"predestined"* to a future *"inheritance."* As 1Peter 1:4 says: We have *"an inheritance that is imperishable, undefiled, and unfading, kept in heaven for you…"* See chapter 15 *"Your Reward in Heaven"* for more on this subject.

- *In him you also, when you heard the word of truth, the gospel of your salvation, and believed in him, were sealed with the promised Holy Spirit, who is the guarantee of our inheritance until we acquire possession of it, to the praise of his glory.*   Ephesians 1:13-14

As we saw in chapter 32, the Holy Spirit teaches us, reminds us, helps our understanding, brings us freedom, and gives us power. The Holy Spirit also is *the guarantee of our inheritance.*

Thank you, God, for blessing us *in the heavenly realms with every spiritual blessing in Christ*!

For Further Reflection

Ephesians 1:1-14: The whole passage on spiritual blessings.

Romans 8:32: Graciously gives us all things.

1Peter 1:3-9: He has given us new birth into a living hope.

****

PART 4
Things God and We Do

There are some things that scripture appears to indicate are shared responsibility. Some verses indicate that God plays a part, and other verses indicate that we are to play a part. It is important that we take an active role in such things, while being aware that God is also involved.

****

Foundations for Eternal Life

Chapter 35
Faith

And Jesus answered them, "Have faith in God." Mark 11:22

For by the grace given to me I say to everyone among you not to think of himself more highly than he ought to think, but to think with sober judgment, each according to the measure of faith that God has assigned. Romans 12:3

"I have declared to both Jews and Greeks that they must turn to God in repentance and have faith in our Lord Jesus." Acts 20:21 NIV

––––––––––––

In chapter 16, we saw that both repentance and faith in Jesus are necessary for salvation. Let's look more closely at faith.

What is faith?

Now faith is being sure of what we hope for and certain of what we do not see. Hebrews 11:1 NIV

From this verse we understand that faith is firm belief in things we can't directly see or touch. It includes believing in future things (*"what we hope for"*) and believing in present spiritual realities (*"what we do not see"*). We see this same duality in Hebrews 11:6:

And without faith it is impossible to please him, for whoever would draw near to God must believe that he exists and that he rewards those who seek him. Hebrews 11:6

This verse indicates that, to please God, we must **believe** both *"that he exists"* (even though we do not see him presently) and that God *"rewards those who seek him"* (something that will happen in the future).

Faith is involved in believing truths revealed in scripture, such as: Jesus is the Son of God; Jesus died for our sins, rose from the dead, and ascended to heaven; and all who turn to God in repentance and have faith in Jesus will be saved.

True faith is accompanied by action. We see this in Hebrews 11, where many people are listed who *"by faith"* did things that pleased God. True faith in Jesus leads people to come to Jesus, trust in Jesus, and follow Jesus. James calls faith that is not accompanied by action *"dead"*:

> *What good is it, my brothers, if someone says he has faith but does not have works? Can that faith save him? If a brother or sister is poorly clothed and lacking in daily food, and one of you says to them, "Go in peace, be warmed and filled," without giving them the things needed for the body, what good is that? So also faith by itself, if it does not have works, is dead.*   James 2:14-17

True faith looks ahead to better things in the life to come, not focusing just on benefits in this life:

> *All these people were still living by faith when they died. They did not receive the things promised; they only saw them and welcomed them from a distance. And they admitted that they were aliens and strangers on earth. People who say such things show that they are looking for a country of their own. If they had been thinking of the country they had left, they would have had opportunity to return. Instead, they were longing for a better country—a heavenly one. Therefore God is not ashamed to be called their God, for he has prepared a city for them.*   Hebrews 11:13-16 NIV

Some benefits of faith are:

- We are saved by God's grace through faith:

> *For by grace you have been saved through faith. And this is not your own doing; it is the gift of God, not a result of works, so that no one may boast.*   Ephesians 2:8-9

- True righteousness comes through faith:

> *For in the gospel a righteousness from God is revealed,*

a righteousness that is by faith from first to last, just as it is written: "The righteous will live by faith."

Romans 1:17 NIV

- We are protected by God's power through faith:

Blessed be the God and Father of our Lord Jesus Christ! According to his great mercy, he has caused us to be born again to a living hope through the resurrection of Jesus Christ from the dead, to an inheritance that is imperishable, undefiled, and unfading, kept in heaven for you, who by God's power are being guarded through faith for a salvation ready to be revealed in the last time. 1Peter 1:3-5

- Faith frees us from fear:

And he awoke and rebuked the wind and said to the sea, "Peace! Be still!" And the wind ceased, and there was a great calm. He said to them, "Why are you so afraid? Have you still no faith?" Mark 4:39-40

In him and through faith in him we may approach God with freedom and confidence. Ephesians 3:12 NIV

- Faith leads to healing, miracles, and spiritual victory:

Jesus turned, and seeing her he said, "Take heart, daughter; your faith has made you well." And instantly the woman was made well. Matthew 9:22

And when Jesus saw their faith, he said to the paralytic, "Son, your sins are forgiven." Mark 2:5

And Jesus answered them, "Truly, I say to you, if you have faith and do not doubt, you will not only do what has been done to the fig tree, but even if you say to this mountain, 'Be taken up and thrown into the sea,' it will happen." Matthew 21:21

For everyone who has been born of God overcomes the world. And this is the victory that has overcome the world—our faith. 1John 5:4

Finally, our faith should be growing over time:

We ought always to thank God for you, brothers, and rightly so, because your faith is growing more and more, and the love every one of you has for each other is increasing. 2Thessalonians 1:3

What about you? Is your faith growing? If not, what should you change in your life so that your faith will grow?

For Further Reflection

Mark 6:1-6: Amazed by their unbelief.

Mark 16:14: Rebuked for unbelief.

Acts 26:18: Sanctified by faith.

Romans 3:20-22: Righteousness from God through faith.

Romans 10:13-17: Faith comes from hearing.

Galatians 2:16: Justified by faith.

Ephesians 6:16: Take up the shield of faith.

Philippians 3:8-11: Righteousness from God by faith.

1Thessalonians 3:9-10: Supply what is lacking in faith.

1Thessalonians 5:8: Putting on faith.

1Timothy 1:18-19: Shipwrecked faith.

1Timothy 6:11-12: Pursue faith.

2Timothy 2:18: Faith destroyed.

2Timothy 2:22: Pursue faith.

Hebrews 11: The faith hall of fame.

Hebrews 12:2: Jesus, the author and perfecter of our faith.

2Peter 1:5-8: Make every effort to add to your faith…

Book Reference: "Beneath Foundations for Eternal Life" by Thomas Edel. Part 2 discusses the nature of faith. A free ebook version may be available at ShalomKoinonia.org.

****

Chapter 36
Hope

May the God of hope fill you with all joy and peace in believing, so that by the power of the Holy Spirit you may abound in hope.   Romans 15:13

Why are you downcast, O my soul? Why so disturbed within me? Put your hope in God, for I will yet praise him, my Savior and my God.   Psalm 42:5, 42:11, 43:5 NIV

Hope has to do with something in the future that we look forward to, but don't yet have. We should distinguish between two kinds of hope:

1. Hope in things that are certain, and
2. Hope in things that are **not** certain.

We often hope for things that are not certain, such as hoping for health and beauty, for increased wealth, or improved relationships. While it's not wrong to hope for these kinds of things, scripture encourages us to put our hope in things that are certain. Let's consider two principles:

FIRST: Our hope should be in God, and in his steadfast love; that he will provide for us and deliver us:

O Israel, hope in the LORD! For with the LORD there is steadfast love, and with him is plentiful redemption.
                                                      Psalm 130:7

...the LORD takes pleasure in those who fear him, in those who hope in his steadfast love.   Psalm 147:11

Command those who are rich in this present world not to be arrogant nor to put their hope in wealth, which is so uncertain, but to put their hope in God, who richly provides us with everything for our enjoyment.
                                                  1Timothy 6:17 NIV

SECOND: Our ultimate hope is for the life to come; eternal life with God, free from the difficulties of this life:

Paul, a servant of God and an apostle of Jesus Christ for the faith of God's elect and the knowledge of the truth that leads to godliness—a faith and knowledge resting on the hope of eternal life, which God, who does not lie, promised before the beginning of time... Titus 1:1-2 NIV

...so that being justified by his grace we might become heirs according to the hope of eternal life. Titus 3:7

If only for this life we have hope in Christ, we are to be pitied more than all men. 1Corinthians 15:19 NIV

What about you? Is your hope in God, in his steadfast love, and in the life to come? Or is your hope in something else?

For Further Reflection

Psalm 33:16-22: Those who hope in his steadfast love.

Psalm 146:5-6: Whose hope is in the LORD his God.

Proverbs 11:7: His hope perishes.

Romans 5:1-5: Suffering produces hope.

Romans 8:22-25: For in this hope we were saved.

Romans 12:12: Rejoice in hope.

Romans 15:4: So that we might have hope.

Romans 15:12-13: Abound with hope.

Ephesians 1:18-19: The hope to which he has called you.

Ephesians 2:11-12: Formerly without hope.

1Thessalonians 1:3: Steadfastness of hope.

1Timothy 4:9-10: Hope in the living God.

Hebrews 6:17-20: Hope as an anchor for the soul.

Hebrews 11:1: Sure of what we hope for.

1Peter 1:3-5: New birth into a living hope.

1John 3:2-3: We shall be like him.

****

Chapter 37
Love

We know that we have passed out of death into life, because we love the brothers. Whoever does not love abides in death.   1John 3:14

Beloved, let us love one another, for love is from God, and whoever loves has been born of God and knows God. Anyone who does not love does not know God, because God is love.   1John 4:7-8

We love because he first loved us.   1John 4:19

And hope does not disappoint us, because God has poured out his love into our hearts by the Holy Spirit, whom he has given us.   Romans 5:5 NIV

In chapters 19 and 20 we focused on the greatest commands: Love God, and love your neighbor. In the context of Jesus' teaching, the emphasis seems to be on our own responsibility to choose to love God and others. However, there is clearly an aspect of our love that is God's doing. As the above verses indicate, our love for one another has its source in God's love, and is tied closely with the salvation he has freely given us.

Love is listed first in describing the *"fruit"* of the Holy Spirit:

> *But the fruit of the Spirit is love, joy, peace, patience, kindness, goodness, faithfulness, gentleness, self-control; against such things there is no law.*
> Galatians 5:22-23

Clearly, without the Holy Spirit we could not love others as we ought to. Likewise, we must abide in Jesus in order to be fruitful:

> *"I am the vine; you are the branches. Whoever abides in me and I in him, he it is that bears much fruit, for apart from me you can do nothing."*   John 15:5

Our love is not yet what it will be, as it should be increasing over time:

> *May the Lord make your love increase and overflow for each other and for everyone else, just as ours does for you.*
> 1Thessalonians 3:12 NIV

> *We ought always to give thanks to God for you, brothers, as is right, because your faith is growing abundantly, and the love of every one of you for one another is increasing.*
> 2Thessalonians 1:3

Loving others is also something we are taught by God to do:

> *Now about brotherly love we do not need to write to you, for you yourselves have been taught by God to love each other.*
> 1Thessalonians 4:9 NIV

We should keep in mind that religious actions that appear to be based on love may actually come from other motives:

> *If I give away all I have, and if I deliver up my body to be burned, but have not love, I gain nothing.*
> 1Corinthians 13:3

What about you? Is love apparent in your life? Is it increasing over time?

For Further Reflection

1Corinthians 13: The Love Chapter. Prayerfully consider what aspect of love you are weakest in. Consider asking God to help you to love others better.

Philippians 1:9-11: Praying for love to abound.

1Timothy 1:7: God gave us a spirit of ... love.

Hebrews 10:24-25: Spur one another on toward love.

1Peter 1:22-23: Sincere brotherly love.

1Peter 4:8: Above all, love...

2Peter 1:5-8: Make every effort to add to your faith... love.

****

Chapter 38
Walk by the Spirit

But I say, walk by the Spirit, and you will not gratify the desires of the flesh. For the desires of the flesh are against the Spirit, and the desires of the Spirit are against the flesh, for these are opposed to each other, to keep you from doing the things you want to do. But if you are led by the Spirit, you are not under the law. Galatians 5:16-18

And those who belong to Christ Jesus have crucified the flesh with its passions and desires. If we live by the Spirit, let us also walk by the Spirit. Let us not become conceited, provoking one another, envying one another. Gal. 5:24-26

God graciously gives the Holy Spirit to his people. This is part of his grace to us (per chapter 32 *"The Gift of the Holy Spirit"*). Yet the above verses indicate that we have a part to play, that we are to *"walk by the Spirit."*

Being "saved" through repentance and faith (chapter 16) does not necessarily result in outward righteousness. There is a process of growing in Christ; of becoming spiritual; of learning to *walk by the Spirit.* Paul speaks of how God's people can be *of the flesh* rather than *spiritual*:

But I, brothers, could not address you as spiritual people, but as people of the flesh, as infants in Christ. I fed you with milk, not solid food, for you were not ready for it. And even now you are not yet ready, for you are still of the flesh. For while there is jealousy and strife among you, are you not of the flesh and behaving only in a human way? 1Corinthians 3:1-3

Walking by the Spirit is not greater self-effort. Nor is it being "controlled" by the Holy Spirit, with us playing no part. Recall from chapter 32 that the Holy Spirit teaches us, reminds us, helps our understanding, brings us freedom, and gives us power. Galatians 5:18 (above) speaks of being *"led by the Spirit,"* as does the book of Romans: *For all who are led by the Spirit of God are sons of God* (Romans 8:14). Being *led by the Spirit* involves choosing to follow the Spirit of God; giving up our own priorities for God's priorities; doing things his way rather than our own way.

A failure to *walk by the Spirit* can result in bondage to sin and other symptoms of spiritual weakness. The apostle Paul discussed his own problem in this area in Romans chapter 7. If you find yourself not doing what you want, but doing the very things you hate (Romans 7:15), then I recommend that you prayerfully consider Romans chapters 5 to 8 (also, consider the books referenced below).

As we *walk by the Spirit,* the *"fruit of the Spirit"* will become apparent in our lives, as discussed in the next chapter. Successfully walking by the Spirit will also result in the practical realization of the truths spoken of in Romans 8:

> *There is therefore now no condemnation for those who are in Christ Jesus. For the law of the Spirit of life has set you free in Christ Jesus from the law of sin and death. For God has done what the law, weakened by the flesh, could not do. By sending his own Son in the likeness of sinful flesh and for sin, he condemned sin in the flesh, in order that the righteous requirement of the law might be fulfilled in us, who walk not according to the flesh but according to the Spirit.*   Romans 8:1-4

Thank you, Lord, for the victory that is ours as we *walk by the Spirit*!

For Further Reflection

Romans 7:1-6: The new way of the Spirit.

Romans 8:1-17: The Spirit and the flesh.

1Corinthians 2:9-16: The Spirit who is from God.

Galatians 3:1-7; 6:7-8: The Spirit, the law, and the flesh.

Book References: "Walking in the Spirit" by Kenneth Berding. "Secret Power" by D.L. Moody (available free on the internet).

****

Chapter 39
Fruit of the Spirit

But the fruit of the Spirit is love, joy, peace, patience, kindness, goodness, faithfulness, gentleness, self-control; against such things there is no law.   Galatians 5:22-23

Therefore, as God's chosen people, holy and dearly loved, clothe yourselves with compassion, kindness, humility, gentleness and patience.   Colossians 3:12 NIV

"Abide in me, and I in you. As the branch cannot bear fruit by itself, unless it abides in the vine, neither can you, unless you abide in me. I am the vine; you are the branches. Whoever abides in me and I in him, he it is that bears much fruit, for apart from me you can do nothing."
        John 15:4-5

By God's grace, as we *walk by the Spirit* the Holy Spirit enables us to bear the *fruit of the Spirit*, as listed in Galatians 5:22-23 above. Many have noted that this passage speaks of the *"fruit" of the Spirit*, not the "fruits" of the Spirit (singular, not plural). The point here is that all of the characteristics listed should be apparent in our lives as we follow Jesus. *The fruit of the Spirit* is not like various abilities (or "gifts") given by God, which are distributed differently to different believers (as discussed in the next chapter). The characteristics listed as *the fruit of the Spirit* should be apparent in every believer's life to some degree.

Scripture contrasts *the fruit of the Spirit* with *the works of the flesh*:

Now the works of the flesh are evident: sexual immorality, impurity, sensuality, idolatry, sorcery, enmity, strife, jealousy, fits of anger, rivalries, dissensions, divisions, envy, drunkenness, orgies, and things like these. I warn you, as I warned you before, that those who do such things will not inherit the

kingdom of God. Galatians 5:19-21

Jesus taught that we can discern false prophets by their fruit:

> *"Beware of false prophets, who come to you in sheep's clothing but inwardly are ravenous wolves. You will recognize them by their fruits. Are grapes gathered from thornbushes, or figs from thistles? So, every healthy tree bears good fruit, but the diseased tree bears bad fruit. A healthy tree cannot bear bad fruit, nor can a diseased tree bear good fruit. Every tree that does not bear good fruit is cut down and thrown into the fire. Thus you will recognize them by their fruits."*
>
> Matthew 7:15-20

Note that it may be difficult to discern a person's fruit from just occasionally observing their public actions. ***The fruit of the Spirit*** is not religious actions, such as giving to the needy, praying, fasting, preaching or prophesying, driving out evil spirits, or performing miracles (see Matthew 6:1-18, 7:21-23). Actions like these may be done by both the saved and the lost, and are not a reliable indicator of true salvation.

What about you? Is your life characterized by ***the fruit of the Spirit***, or by ***the works of the flesh***?

For Further Reflection

Matt. 12:33-37: Make a tree good and its fruit will be good.

Luke 6:43-45: Each tree is recognized by its own fruit.

Luke 13:6-9: He went to find fruit.

John 15:1-8: The branch cannot bear fruit by itself.

Romans 7:4-6: Bear fruit for God.

Ephesians 5:8-12: The fruit of light.

Philippians 1:9-11: Filled with the fruit of righteousness.

Colossians 1:9-12: Bearing fruit in every good work.

James 3:17-18: Full of mercy and good fruits.

****

Chapter 40
Different Gifts

We have different gifts, according to the grace given us. If a man's gift is prophesying, let him use it in proportion to his faith. If it is serving, let him serve; if it is teaching, let him teach; if it is encouraging, let him encourage; if it is contributing to the needs of others, let him give generously; if it is leadership, let him govern diligently; if it is showing mercy, let him do it cheerfully. Romans 12:6-8 NIV

Each one should use whatever gift he has received to serve others, faithfully administering God's grace in its various forms. 1Peter 4:10 NIV

God gives various abilities (or "gifts") to his people. But it is up to each of us to humbly serve others with the abilities God has given each of us.

Unfortunately, having God-given abilities does not necessarily correlate with spiritual maturity. The church at Corinth appears to be well-endowed with spiritual gifts (1Corinthians 1:7; 12:4-31, 14:1-40), yet Paul writes to them:

But I, brothers, could not address you as spiritual people, but as people of the flesh, as infants in Christ. I fed you with milk, not solid food, for you were not ready for it. And even now you are not yet ready, for you are still of the flesh. For while there is jealousy and strife among you, are you not of the flesh and behaving only in a human way? 1Corinthians 3:1-3

God-given gifts can easily become a source of sinful pride. Paul also writes to the Corinthians:

For who makes you different from anyone else? What do you have that you did not receive? And if you did receive it, why do you boast as though you did not? 1Corinthians 4:7 NIV

Some gifts from God are generally perceived to be more important than other gifts. Scripture uses the analogy of a human body to emphasize the value of each person and their gifting within the body of Christ:

> *The eye cannot say to the hand, "I have no need of you," nor again the head to the feet, "I have no need of you." On the contrary, the parts of the body that seem to be weaker are indispensable, and on those parts of the body that we think less honorable we bestow the greater honor, and our unpresentable parts are treated with greater modesty, which our more presentable parts do not require. But God has so composed the body, giving greater honor to the part that lacked it, that there may be no division in the body, but that the members may have the same care for one another.* 1Corinthians 12:21-25

Scripture emphasizes the need for God's people to serve one another in love. Without love, our gifts are of no benefit:

> *If I speak in the tongues of men and of angels, but have not love, I am a noisy gong or a clanging cymbal. And if I have prophetic powers, and understand all mysteries and all knowledge, and if I have all faith, so as to remove mountains, but have not love, I am nothing. If I give away all I have, and if I deliver up my body to be burned, but have not love, I gain nothing.*
> 1Corinthians 13:1-3

For Further Reflection

Ask God for discernment to understand the gift (or gifts) he has given you, and how to best serve others.

Exodus 31:1-6: God gives the ability.

Deuteronomy 8:17-18: God gives the ability.

1Corinth. 12:4 to 13:3: Different gifts, service, workings.

1Corinthians 14:1-40: Proper use of spiritual gifts.

****

Chapter 41
Laying on of Hands

Therefore let us leave the elementary teachings about Christ and go on to maturity, not laying again the foundation of repentance from acts that lead to death, and of faith in God, instruction about baptisms, the laying on of hands, the resurrection of the dead, and eternal judgment. And God permitting, we will do so. Hebrews 6:1-3 NIV

This is one of the last chapters added to this book... I didn't want to deal with this subject. Scripture, in my opinion, is not very clear regarding *"laying on of hands."* I wanted to keep this book limited to simple and clear subjects, subjects that I think I understand reasonably well. However, the author of Hebrews lists this subject as one of *"the elementary teachings about Christ"* and part of our *"foundation"* (Hebrews 6:1-3). We have already covered the other subjects listed in Hebrews 6:1-3. If scripture calls *laying on of hands* elementary and foundational, then it is.

Here is the only New Testament instruction I am aware of regarding *laying on of hands*:

> *Do not be hasty in the laying on of hands, nor take part in the sins of others; keep yourself pure.* 1Timothy 5:22

Scripture gives us several good examples of laying on hands. The practice is associated with healing, receiving a spiritual gift, commissioning people for service, or imparting some other grace from God. Here are some scriptural examples:

> *"When you bring the Levites before the LORD, the people of Israel shall lay their hands on the Levites, and Aaron shall offer the Levites before the LORD as a wave offering from the people of Israel, that they may do the service of the LORD."* Numbers 8:10-11

And Moses did as the LORD commanded him. He took Joshua and made him stand before Eleazar the priest and the whole congregation, and he laid his hands on him and commissioned him as the LORD directed through Moses.
Numbers 27:22-23

And Joshua the son of Nun was full of the spirit of wisdom, for Moses had laid his hands on him. So the people of Israel obeyed him and did as the LORD had commanded Moses.
Deuteronomy 34:9

He could not do any miracles there, except lay his hands on a few sick people and heal them.
Mark 6:5 NIV

When the sun was setting, the people brought to Jesus all who had various kinds of sickness, and laying his hands on each one, he healed them.
Luke 4:40 NIV

And what they said pleased the whole gathering, and they chose Stephen, a man full of faith and of the Holy Spirit, and Philip, and Prochorus, and Nicanor, and Timon, and Parmenas, and Nicolaus, a proselyte of Antioch. These they set before the apostles, and they prayed and laid their hands on them.
Acts 6:5-6

Then Peter and John placed their hands on them, and they received the Holy Spirit.
Acts 8:17 NIV

Do not neglect your gift, which was given you through a prophetic message when the body of elders laid their hands on you.
1Timothy 4:14 NIV

For this reason I remind you to fan into flame the gift of God, which is in you through the laying on of my hands.
2Timothy 1:6 NIV

For Further Reflection

Ask God for wisdom regarding the proper use of *"laying on of hands."*

****

PART 5
Things We Should NOT Do

Just as there are things God calls us to **DO**, as discussed in Part 2, there are things God calls his people to **NOT DO**.

This is a somewhat awkward subject, because part of being saved is no longer being under law. We no longer live our lives simply based on "Do this" or "Don't do that!" We are called to walk by the Spirit, not the law. Yet, the New Testament clearly indicates actions that are inconsistent with following Jesus. If your life is characterized by things that are contrary to salvation, then it may be that you aren't yet saved, or that there is a serious failure in your spiritual walk that needs to be remedied.

****

Chapter 42
Not by Works, Not by Law

For by grace you have been saved through faith. And this is not your own doing; it is the gift of God, not a result of works, so that no one may boast. Ephesians 2:8-9

Therefore no one will be declared righteous in his sight by observing the law; rather, through the law we become conscious of sin. Romans 3:20 NIV

It is part of our fallen nature to want to somehow earn salvation; to somehow be worthy of eternal life based on our own goodness or effort. This concept is completely contrary to the salvation we have in Jesus. Our salvation is a gift from God. No one has ever been worthy of it. No one has ever earned it.

This is precisely what sets salvation through Jesus apart from other "religions." Other religions involve self-improvement and good works to become acceptable to God, or to somehow transcend this life and become something better.

Followers of Jesus, on the other hand, come to God without relying on any goodness of their own. We receive forgiveness and salvation from God as a free gift made possible by Jesus' sacrifice for our sins. We are made righteous by God, through being born again and the gift of the Holy Spirit, not by our own self-effort. We learn to cease from our own striving, and learn to rest in God and trust in him:

But now a righteousness from God, apart from law, has been made known, to which the Law and the Prophets testify. This righteousness from God comes through faith in Jesus Christ to all who believe. There is no difference, for all have sinned and fall short of the glory of God, and are justified freely by his grace through the

redemption that came by Christ Jesus.

Romans 3:21-24 NIV

But there is often a problem. We tend to fall back into a religious mode of trying to please God by following his commands by our own effort. This can lead us back into bondage to sin. Paul describes this problem in his own life:

> *I was once alive apart from the law, but when the commandment came, sin came alive and I died. The very commandment that promised life proved to be death to me. For sin, seizing an opportunity through the commandment, deceived me and through it killed me.*

Romans 7:9-11

The solution is to learn to ***walk by the Spirit***:

> *But I say, walk by the Spirit, and you will not gratify the desires of the flesh. For the desires of the flesh are against the Spirit, and the desires of the Spirit are against the flesh, for these are opposed to each other, to keep you from doing the things you want to do. But if you are led by the Spirit, you are not under the law.*

Galatians 5:16-18

This is key to living for Jesus: learning to ***walk by the Spirit***. To better understand how to ***walk by the Spirit***, prayerfully consider the verses below, under *"For Further Reflection,"* and review chapter 38 *"Walk by the Spirit."*

What about you? Have you tried to please God simply by following rules by your own strength?

For Further Reflection

Romans 3:9 to 4:25: Righteousness through faith.

Romans 6:1 to 8:17: Life by the Spirit.

Galatians 1:1 to 6:18: People are rebuked for relying on circumcision and the law rather than faith in Jesus.

Revelation 2:1-7: Good works without love.

* * * * * * * * * * * *

Chapter 43
Treasures on Earth

"Do not lay up for yourselves treasures on earth, where moth and rust destroy and where thieves break in and steal, but lay up for yourselves treasures in heaven, where neither moth nor rust destroys and where thieves do not break in and steal. For where your treasure is, there your heart will be also."   Matthew 6:19-21

"Fear not, little flock, for it is your Father's good pleasure to give you the kingdom. Sell your possessions, and give to the needy. Provide yourselves with moneybags that do not grow old, with a treasure in the heavens that does not fail, where no thief approaches and no moth destroys. For where your treasure is, there will your heart be also."
Luke 12:32-34

Jesus calls us to use worldly wealth for eternal purposes; to **not** store it up for selfish purposes. Scripture condemns those who are wealthy when they use their wealth and power for selfish purposes (James 5:1-6). Those who are rich are instructed to do otherwise:

> *As for the rich in this present age, charge them not to be haughty, nor to set their hopes on the uncertainty of riches, but on God, who richly provides us with everything to enjoy. They are to do good, to be rich in good works, to be generous and ready to share, thus storing up treasure for themselves as a good foundation for the future, so that they may take hold of that which is truly life.* 1Timothy 6:17-19

For myself, I find this subject of wealth management very difficult to balance properly. On one hand we have verses that emphasize the need to trust God for our needs, such as:

> *"Therefore do not be anxious, saying, 'What shall we eat?' or 'What shall we drink?' or 'What shall we*

wear?' For the Gentiles seek after all these things, and your heavenly Father knows that you need them all. But seek first the kingdom of God and his righteousness, and all these things will be added to you."

Matthew 6:31-33

Other verses emphasize the importance of work:

But if anyone does not provide for his relatives, and especially for members of his household, he has denied the faith and is worse than an unbeliever.   1Timothy 5:8

For even when we were with you, we would give you this command: If anyone is not willing to work, let him not eat.

2Thessalonians 3:10

And some verses speak of the wisdom of some types of storage:

In the house of the wise are stores of choice food and oil, but a foolish man devours all he has.   Prov. 21:20 NIV

Go to the ant, you sluggard; consider its ways and be wise! It has no commander, no overseer or ruler, yet it stores its provisions in summer and gathers its food at harvest.

Proverbs 6:6-8 NIV

For Further Reflection

Proverbs 6:9-11: How long will you lie there?

Proverbs 30:7-9: Give me neither poverty nor riches.

Matthew 6:19-34: Do not be anxious about tomorrow.

Luke 12:13-34: Be on your guard against all kinds of greed.

Luke 16:1-15: The shrewd manager.

2Corinthians 9:6-11: You will be enriched in every way.

1Thessalonians 4:11-12: Work with your hands.

2Thessalonians 3:10-12: Earn your own bread.

1Timothy 6:6-10: Be content.

Hebrews 13:5: Be content with what you have.

1John 1:9: If we confess our sins…

****

Chapter 44
Sexual Immorality

It is God's will that you should be sanctified: that you should avoid sexual immorality; that each of you should learn to control his own body in a way that is holy and honorable, not in passionate lust like the heathen, who do not know God; and that in this matter no one should wrong his brother or take advantage of him. The Lord will punish men for all such sins, as we have already told you and warned you. For God did not call us to be impure, but to live a holy life.   1Thessalonians 4:3-7 NIV

Speaking frankly, the area of sexual purity has probably been the most difficult area of my life to deal with. I suppose I am "normal" in this regard by many measures. However, I think I have more difficulties than some men, due to allowing my mind to follow after immoral fantasies before I chose to follow Jesus (and occasionally thereafter!). By the same reasoning, my difficulties are probably less than many others who have participated more directly in sexual sin.

Paul apparently had a gift of celibacy, yet he was able to sympathize with those of us who don't:

I wish that all were as I myself am. But each has his own gift from God, one of one kind and one of another.

To the unmarried and the widows I say that it is good for them to remain single as I am. But if they cannot exercise self-control, they should marry. For it is better to marry than to burn with passion.   1Corinthians 7:7-9

Paul acknowledges that it is **not abnormal** for followers of Jesus to "**burn with passion**" and to have difficulty controlling themselves. Our sexual desires are part of how God made us. Many, perhaps most, followers of Jesus are not able to simply turn their sexual desires off. God made us with such desires to promote marriages and families. Satan seeks to twist those God-given desires to lead us into sin.

While a good marriage relationship is the preferred means of sexual fulfillment, that is not an immediate option for many people. For those who are not married, or are not with their spouse (due to circumstances or relational problems), if you are able to control yourself in this area, then thank God for a gift of self-control. For those who have more difficulty, it appears to me that scripture does not condemn self-gratification. While self-gratification can be done in ways that are sinful, I don't believe that it is inherently sinful. Ask God to show you how to live in a way that is pleasing to him.

I believe that there are degrees of sin (based on verses such as Genesis 18:20-21, Exodus 32:30-31, 1Samuel 2:17, Mark 3:28-29, and John 19:11). I believe it is a greater sin to physically commit adultery than it is to look at someone with lust, even though both are a form of adultery (Matthew 5:27-28). It is a greater sin to actually seduce someone than to merely think about it. It is a greater sin to murder someone than to just hate them. Don't allow the idea that "all sins are equal" to lead you into ever-greater sins. Don't use that idea to justify actually doing something you've only thought about doing.

Many can testify that lesser sins tend to lead to greater sins. Softcore pornography leads to hardcore porn, which leads to even worse sin. ***Flee from sexual immorality!*** (1Cor. 6:18).

For Further Reflection

Genesis 18:16-19:28: They looked down toward Sodom.
Numbers 25:1-18: While Israel was staying in Shittim...
John 8:1-11: The woman caught in adultery.
Romans 1:18-32: The wrath of God is being revealed...
1Corinthians 5:1-13: It is actually reported...
1Corinthians 6:9-20: Honor God with your body.
1John 1:9: If we confess our sins...

****

Chapter 45
Pride

Pride goes before destruction, and a haughty spirit before a fall.   Proverbs 16:18

Do you see a man who is wise in his own eyes? There is more hope for a fool than for him.   Proverbs 26:12

Live in harmony with one another. Do not be haughty, but associate with the lowly. Never be wise in your own sight.
Romans 12:16

The issue of pride has been another difficult area for me personally to overcome. This is a difficult sin to deal with, partly because "pride" is not always bad (as used in the English language). Some types of boasting and pride are okay, while other types aren't. Here are some examples of the good kind:

Each one should test his own actions. Then he can take pride in himself, without comparing himself to somebody else, for each one should carry his own load.
Galatians 6:4-5 NIV

Therefore, as it is written: "Let him who boasts boast in the Lord."   1Corinthians 1:31 NIV

One simple definition of the bad kind of pride (sinful pride) is this: to think of yourself more highly than you ought to. This is usually accompanied by thinking less of others than you ought to. As scripture says:

For by the grace given to me I say to everyone among you not to think of himself more highly than he ought to think, but to think with sober judgment, each according to the measure of faith that God has assigned.
Romans 12:3

Do nothing out of selfish ambition or vain conceit, but

in humility consider others better than yourselves.
Philippians 2:3 NIV

Pride appears to be the root sin that led to the devil's downfall. Pride may have been the first sin in all creation (even ahead of Adam and Eve in Genesis 3):

"Your heart was proud because of your beauty; you corrupted your wisdom for the sake of your splendor. I cast you to the ground; I exposed you before kings, to feast their eyes on you."
Ezekiel 28:17

He must not be a recent convert, or he may become puffed up with conceit and fall into the condemnation of the devil.
1Timothy 3:6

Humility is widely understood to be the opposite of pride:

Clothe yourselves, all of you, with humility toward one another, for "God opposes the proud but gives grace to the humble."
1Peter 5:5

He mocks proud mockers but gives grace to the humble.
Proverbs 3:34 NIV

When pride comes, then comes disgrace, but with the humble is wisdom.
Proverbs 11:2

What about you? Are you proud or humble?

For Further Reflection

2Chronicles 26:16-21: King Uzziah's pride.

Psalm 10:4-6: In his pride the wicked does not seek him...

Proverbs 18:12: Before his downfall...

Jeremiah 9:23-24: Let not the wise man boast...

Ezekiel 28:12-19: The devil's downfall.

Daniel 4:1-37: King Nebuchadnezzar's pride.

1Corinthians 1:17-31: So that no one may boast.

1John 1:9: If we confess our sins...

****

Chapter 46
Revenge

Do not say, "I will do to him as he has done to me;
I will pay the man back for what he has done."
Proverbs 24:29

Do not take revenge, my friends, but leave room for God's
wrath, for it is written: "It is mine to avenge; I will repay,"
says the Lord.   Romans 12:19 NIV

In chapter 22 we looked at the importance of forgiving others. A failure to forgive tends to result in a desire for revenge. It seems to me that seeking revenge is the opposite of forgiveness.

Consider a larger section of Romans 12:

Do not repay anyone evil for evil. Be careful to do what
is right in the eyes of everybody. If it is possible, as far
as it depends on you, live at peace with everyone. Do not
take revenge, my friends, but leave room for God's
wrath, for it is written: "It is mine to avenge; I will
repay," says the Lord. On the contrary: "If your enemy
is hungry, feed him; if he is thirsty, give him something
to drink. In doing this, you will heap burning coals on
his head." Do not be overcome by evil, but overcome
evil with good.   Romans 12:17-21 NIV

Taking revenge also involves a failure to love others. When the command to *"love your neighbor as yourself"* was first given, it was associated with not seeking revenge:

"You shall not take vengeance or bear a grudge against
the sons of your own people, but you shall love your
neighbor as yourself: I am the LORD."   Leviticus 19:18

Peter also raises this issue of taking revenge:

Do not repay evil for evil or reviling for reviling, but on the contrary, bless, for to this you were called, that you may obtain a blessing.
1Peter 3:9

It is somewhat intriguing that God appears to reserve judgment and revenge for himself:

"It is mine to avenge; I will repay," says the Lord.
Romans 12:19 NIV

Perhaps that is because God is the only one whose knowledge is sufficient to rightly judge and repay people. Our own judgments about others tend to be warped by our own selfishness and ignorance.

Jesus gives us a challenging example of forgiveness rather than vengeance:

And when they came to the place that is called The Skull, there they crucified him, and the criminals, one on his right and one on his left. And Jesus said, "Father, forgive them, for they know not what they do."
Luke 23:33-34

What about you? What was your response the last time someone wronged you? Vengeance or forgiveness?

For Further Reflection

Judges 15:1-20: Samson's revenge.

Proverbs 20:22: Do not say, "I will repay evil."

Matthew 5:38-48: Eye for eye, and tooth for tooth.

Acts 7:59-60: Stephen's prayer.

2Thessalonians 1:5-10: God is just: He will pay back…

2Timothy 4:14-15: The Lord will repay…

1John 1:9: If we confess our sins…

✳✳✳✳✳✳✳✳✳✳✳

Chapter 47
Quarreling

Remind them of these things, and charge them before God not to quarrel about words, which does no good, but only ruins the hearers.   2Timothy 2:14

Have nothing to do with foolish, ignorant controversies; you know that they breed quarrels. And the Lord's servant must not be quarrelsome but kind to everyone, able to teach, patiently enduring evil, correcting his opponents with gentleness. God may perhaps grant them repentance leading to a knowledge of the truth, and they may come to their senses and escape from the snare of the devil, after being captured by him to do his will.   2Timothy 2:23-26

It is intriguing to me how followers of Jesus often strongly disagree on various subjects, especially spiritual subjects. I take this to be evidence of just how much our own experience and culture impact how we understand things, and just how imperfect our understanding is. Based on the many differing beliefs that many genuine followers of Jesus hold to, I conclude that our understanding is not as inspired by the Holy Spirit as we may think it is!

Scripture says:

Now we see but a poor reflection as in a mirror; then we shall see face to face. Now I know in part; then I shall know fully, even as I am fully known.
1Corinthians 13:12 NIV

For by the grace given to me I say to everyone among you not to think of himself more highly than he ought to think, but to think with sober judgment, each according to the measure of faith that God has assigned.
Romans 12:3

We tend to think of ourselves and our own knowledge more highly than we ought to. This can lead believers into arguments and quarrels that are not beneficial. Consider some additional verses regarding our speech:

> *When words are many, sin is not absent, but he who holds his tongue is wise.*   Proverbs 10:19 NIV

> *Let no corrupting talk come out of your mouths, but only such as is good for building up, as fits the occasion, that it may give grace to those who hear.*   Ephesians 4:29

> *Know this, my beloved brothers: let every person be quick to hear, slow to speak, slow to anger; for the anger of man does not produce the righteousness of God.*
> James 1:19-20

What about you? Have you quarreled with someone recently? What was the outcome?

For Further Reflection

Matthew 12:33-37: Out of the overflow of the heart...

Luke 6:45: For out of the overflow of his heart...

Romans 16:17-18: Watch out for those who cause divisions.

Titus 3:9-11: Avoid foolish controversies.

James 1:26: A tight rein on his tongue.

James 3:1-18: The tongue is a fire.

1John 1:9: If we confess our sins...

****

Chapter 48
Keep on Sinning

No one born of God makes a practice of sinning, for God's seed abides in him, and he cannot keep on sinning because he has been born of God.

1John 3:9

We know that we have come to know him if we obey his commands. The man who says, "I know him," but does not do what he commands is a liar, and the truth is not in him.

1John 2:3-4 NIV

The above verses clearly indicate that true salvation results in changed actions. Unfortunately, many followers of Jesus emphasize salvation by God's **grace** so much that they don't seem to have any expectation of lives changing as a result of salvation. Because of this, I believe many people who aren't truly saved are deceived into believing otherwise.

For John, a test of true salvation isn't having some spiritual gift, having a special spiritual experience, or saying the right spiritual words. For John, a primary evidence of salvation is obedience to God. Consider John's statement again:

We know that we have come to know him if we obey his commands. The man who says, "I know him," but does not do what he commands is a liar, and the truth is not in him.

1John 2:3-4 NIV

The author of Hebrews also addresses the issue of obedience:

If we deliberately keep on sinning after we have received the knowledge of the truth, no sacrifice for sins is left, but only a fearful expectation of judgment and of raging fire that will consume the enemies of God.

Hebrews 10:26-27 NIV

Paul also addresses this issue:

Do you not know that the wicked will not inherit the kingdom of God? Do not be deceived: Neither the sexually immoral nor idolaters nor adulterers nor male prostitutes nor homosexual offenders nor thieves nor the greedy nor drunkards nor slanderers nor swindlers will inherit the kingdom of God. And that is what some of you were. But you were washed, you were sanctified, you were justified in the name of the Lord Jesus Christ and by the Spirit of our God. 1Corinthians 6:9-11 NIV

I am not claiming that followers of Jesus are perfect and never sin. But I am saying that sin should be the exception in our lives, not the norm, especially the longer we know Jesus. As John also writes:

My dear children, I write this to you so that you will not sin. But if anybody does sin, we have one who speaks to the Father in our defense—Jesus Christ, the Righteous One. He is the atoning sacrifice for our sins, and not only for ours but also for the sins of the whole world.
1John 2:1-2 NIV

What about you? Is your life characterized by obedience to God, or obedience to sin? If your life is still characterized by obedience to sin rather than obedience to God, then I encourage you to revisit chapter 16 (*What Must I Do to Be Saved?*), chapter 27 (*Obey*), chapter 30 (*Set Free From Sin*), chapter 38 (*Walk by the Spirit*), and chapter 42 (*Not by Works, Not by Law*).

For Further Reflection

Matthew 7:21-27: "Lord, Lord..."
Luke 6:46-49: "Why do you call me 'Lord, Lord'..."
Romans 6:1-23: Shall we go on sinning?
1Corinthians 5:9-11: With such a man do not even eat.
Galatians 5:19-26: The works of the flesh.
Galatians 6:1: If someone is caught in a sin.
Galatians 6:7-10: You will reap what you sow.
1Peter 1:14-16: Be holy.
1Peter 2:11-12: Abstain from sinful desires.

****

PART 6
Things God Doesn't Do

Some things are contrary to God's nature, and God simply doesn't do those things. While these things should be obvious, it is surprisingly easy for us to think and act otherwise. Understanding these things should strengthen our trust in God.

****

Chapter 49
Do Wrong, Pervert Justice

It is unthinkable that God would do wrong,
that the Almighty would pervert justice.
Job 34:12 NIV

God has never done wrong or perverted justice, and he never will. Still, we tend to blame God for our problems.

When Job's life went from being very good to losing everything, Job's wife said to him:

"Are you still holding on to your integrity? Curse God and die!"   Job 2:9 NIV

It is our natural sinful tendency to blame God for our problems. Often, our problems are self-inflicted; often we are simply reaping what we've sown; yet we blame God.

Other times, such as in Job's case, our problems are largely caused by others, and we still tend to blame God. Job is a marvelous example of patience in the face of suffering, but he also tended to find fault with God:

"I cry out to you, O God, but you do not answer; I stand up, but you merely look at me. You turn on me ruthlessly; with the might of your hand you attack me. You snatch me up and drive me before the wind; you toss me about in the storm."   Job 30:20-22 NIV

God had not attacked Job. It is clear from the first two chapters of Job that God had temporarily stopped protecting Job, and that it was actually Satan who had attacked Job. Job, however, was not aware of this, and he accused God of attacking him.

Whatever your circumstances are, if you are a follower of Jesus, remember:

And we know that in all things God works for the good

of those who love him, who have been called according to his purpose. Romans 8:28 NIV

He who did not spare his own Son but gave him up for us all, how will he not also with him graciously give us all things? Romans 8:32

God is light, and in him is no darkness at all. 1John 1:5

Life here on earth can be very difficult, and often there isn't much we can do to change that. Our trials may continue for what seems to be a very long time. The prophet Habakkuk foresaw that God would send the Babylonian army against his own country. He had to deal with how to trust and follow God when his world was about to fall apart. Part of his conclusion was:

Though the fig tree does not bud and there are no grapes on the vines, though the olive crop fails and the fields produce no food, though there are no sheep in the pen and no cattle in the stalls, yet I will rejoice in the LORD, I will be joyful in God my Savior. Habakkuk 3:17-18 NIV

What about you? Will you *rejoice in the LORD*, and *be joyful in God*, regardless of your circumstances?

For Further Reflection

Have you ever blamed God for your problems? Should you apologize?

Psalm 10:1-18: Why, O LORD, do you stand far off?

Proverbs 3:11-12: Do not despise the LORD's discipline.

2Corinthians 4:16-17: Our light and momentary troubles.

Titus 1:1-2: God does not lie.

Hebrews 6:16-18: It is impossible for God to lie.

Hebrews 12:3-11: Discipline from God.

Hebrews 13:5-6: "I will never leave you…"

****

PART 7
Putting it All Together

Up to this point we have looked at foundations for eternal life by looking at various "things":

PART 1: Things We Know

PART 2: Things We Do

PART 3: Things God Does

PART 4: Things God and We Do

PART 5: Things We Should NOT Do

PART 6: Things God Doesn't Do

While all of these "things" are important to various degrees, what is ultimately important is using our understanding of these things to enter into salvation and to continue to live in that salvation in a way that is pleasing to God.

In this section we will look at salvation from three different viewpoints:

- We will review various aspects of salvation.

- To be saved is to be "in Christ."

- Salvation involves coming to Jesus, being reconciled to God, and knowing and loving God.

We will then close with the need to "stand firm."

****

Chapter 50
Salvation

"For the Son of Man came to seek and to save the lost."
Luke 19:10

Here is a trustworthy saying that deserves full acceptance: Christ Jesus came into the world to save sinners—of whom I am the worst.
1Timothy 1:15 NIV

"For God so loved the world that he gave his one and only Son, that whoever believes in him shall not perish but have eternal life. For God did not send his Son into the world to condemn the world, but to save the world through him."
John 3:16-17 NIV

Jesus came to **save sinners**, to **seek and to save the lost**. That includes you and me. It seems to me that a primary theme of the entire Bible is God's provision of salvation to mankind. Another primary theme is the rejection of salvation by most people. God has provided a way of salvation for me and for you. Let us be careful to not reject it!

What does it mean to be saved? What does "salvation" look like? God is the one who has initiated salvation, and God freely provides us with the many blessings and provisions of salvation. Many aspects of salvation have been discussed throughout this book:

- Salvation is necessary because of our own spiritual death caused by sin (chapter 3).

- Jesus died for our sins, making salvation possible (ch. 4).

- Jesus rose from the dead, proving his power over death and his power to save us from our sins (chapter 5).

- Salvation has its source in God's love (chapter 6).

- Knowledge about God and creation helps us to understand salvation (chapters 1 to 15).

- Salvation involves coming to Jesus, trusting in Jesus, and following Jesus. Each of us must turn to God in repentance and have faith in Jesus (chapter 16).

- Salvation includes many blessings and provisions from God during this life: Our sins are forgiven; we are set free from sin's power; we are born of God; the gift of the Holy Spirit; we are members of one body; and we are given every spiritual blessing in Christ! (chapters 28-34).

- Love for God affects how we live: things we do (chapters 17 to 27, & 35 to 41) and things we avoid (chapters 42 to 48). We are able to live a righteous life only because of God's many blessings and provisions (chapters 28 to 41).

- Future blessings are included: no condemnation on the day of judgment, and future reward (chapters 14 and 15).

Consider again this marvelous salvation:

But when the goodness and loving kindness of God our Savior appeared, he saved us, not because of works done by us in righteousness, but according to his own mercy, by the washing of regeneration and renewal of the Holy Spirit, whom he poured out on us richly through Jesus Christ our Savior, so that being justified by his grace we might become heirs according to the hope of eternal life.
Titus 3:4-7

Thank you, God, for such a great salvation!

For Further Reflection

Acts 4:8-12: There is salvation in no one else.

Romans 1:16-17: The power of God for salvation.

2Corinthians 6:1-2: Now is the day of salvation.

2Corinthians 7:8-10: Repentance that leads to salvation.

Titus 2:11-14: The grace of God that brings salvation.

Hebrews 2:1-4: If we neglect such a great salvation.

Book Reference: "The Normal Christian Life" by Watchman Nee.

****

Chapter 51
In Christ

Therefore, if anyone is in Christ, he is a new creation. The old has passed away; behold, the new has come.

2Corinthians 5:17

There is therefore now no condemnation for those who are in Christ Jesus.

Romans 8:1

Peace to all of you who are in Christ.

1Peter 5:14

Scripture refers to those who are saved as being *"in Christ."* If you are *"in Christ,"* you are *a new creation; the old has passed away, the new has come*! You have a new identity. This is part of God's grace; something God does:

And it is God who establishes us with you <u>in Christ</u>, and has anointed us, and who has also put his seal on us and given us his Spirit in our hearts as a guarantee.

2Corinthians 1:21-22

Understanding our new identity *in Christ* is an important key to following Jesus. Our position *in Christ* is what aligns us with God's grace, the many blessings freely given by God.

We have already looked at many of the blessings that are ours by God's grace, if we are *in Christ* (chapters 28 to 34):

- Because Jesus shed his blood, our sins are forgiven.
- Because Jesus died, we are set free from sin.
- Because Jesus rose from the dead, we have new life.
- Because Jesus is exalted, the Holy Spirit is poured out.
- We are members of one body, the body of Christ.
- God has given us every spiritual blessing *in Christ*.

Let's consider a few more verses related to being *in Christ*:

There is therefore now no condemnation for those who are <u>in Christ Jesus</u>. For the law of the Spirit of life has set you free <u>in Christ Jesus</u> from the law of sin and death.

Romans 8:1-2

But now that faith has come, we are no longer under a guardian, for <u>in Christ Jesus</u> you are all sons of God, through faith. Galatians 3:25-26

For we are his workmanship, created <u>in Christ Jesus</u> for good works, which God prepared beforehand, that we should walk in them. Ephesians 2:10

But now <u>in Christ Jesus</u> you who once were far off have been brought near by the blood of Christ.

Ephesians 2:13

These verses clarify some more blessings we have if we are *in Christ*:

- We are no longer condemned.
- We are set free from the law of sin and death.
- We are all sons of God through faith.
- We are God's workmanship, created to do good works.
- We have been brought near to God.

One of our enemy's greatest deceptions is to keep believers from understanding their new identity *"in Christ,"* so they'll continue to live like unsaved people. Don't fall for it! God has greatly blessed us, his people. Let's live in that blessing!

For you were once darkness, but now you are light in the Lord. Live as children of light... Ephesians 5:8 NIV

For Further Reflection

Read the 11 bullet points above aloud, making them personal (for example, change "our" to "my" and "we are" to "I am").

Ephesians 1:3-14: Every spiritual blessing in Christ.

Philippians 1:1; Colossians 1:2: To those who are in Christ.

1John 3:1-3: We are called children of God!

Book Reference: "Victory Over the Darkness" by Neil Anderson; "Realizing the power of your identity in Christ."

****

Chapter 52
"Come to Me"

"Come to me, all who labor and are heavy laden, and I will give you rest. Take my yoke upon you, and learn from me, for I am gentle and lowly in heart, and you will find rest for your souls. For my yoke is easy, and my burden is light."

Matthew 11:28-30

"If anyone thirsts, let him come to me and drink. Whoever believes in me, as the Scripture has said, 'Out of his heart will flow rivers of living water.'"   John 7:37-38

Jesus invites each of us to come to him. This is an invitation to salvation: *"Come to me."* How do we come to Jesus? We come to Jesus through repentance and faith (per chapter 16).

Salvation is not primarily a matter of things we know, or things we do; salvation is a matter of right relationship:

"And this is eternal life, that they know you the only true God, and Jesus Christ whom you have sent."   John 17:3

Eternal life involves knowing God. Sin had broken our relationship with God. Through the death of Jesus our relationship with God is restored; we are *reconciled* to God:

For if, when we were God's enemies, we were reconciled to him through the death of his Son, how much more, having been reconciled, shall we be saved through his life! Not only is this so, but we also rejoice in God through our Lord Jesus Christ, through whom we have now received reconciliation.   Romans 5:10-11 NIV

To help us understand salvation, this book has broken down spiritual concepts into categories such as *"Things We Know"* and *"Things We Do."* However, it is a mistake to think that salvation is just a matter of things to know and things to do. Just knowing spiritual truth and doing religious things does not save us. Rather, salvation involves coming to Jesus, trusting in Jesus, and following Jesus. We come to Jesus to be *reconciled* to God and to *know* the Father and the Son.

Once we are reconciled to God through Jesus, we should learn things and do things that strengthen our relationship with God. We should avoid things that hurt our relationship with God. That is the point of writing about *"Things We Know," "Things We Do,"* and *"Things We Should NOT Do."* The goal is to know God better; to deepen our relationship with God; to deepen our love for God.

Have you already come to Jesus for salvation? If so, I urge you to **grow in the grace and knowledge of our Lord and Savior Jesus Christ. To him be glory both now and forever! Amen.** (2Peter 3:18 NIV)

If you have not yet come to Jesus, why not do so today?

> **Behold, now is the favorable time; behold, now is the day of salvation.** 2Corinthians 6:2

> **The Spirit and the bride say, "Come!" And let him who hears say, "Come!" Whoever is thirsty, let him come; and whoever wishes, let him take the free gift of the water of life.** Revelation 22:17 NIV

For Further Reflection

Matthew 7:21-23: "I never knew you."

Matthew 19:13-15: Let the little children come.

John 3:19-21: Coming to the light.

John 5:39-40: Refusing to come to Jesus.

John 6:35-51: "Whoever comes to me shall not hunger."

John 14:6: Coming to the Father through Jesus.

2Corinthians 5:17-21: Reconciled to God through Jesus.

Philippians 3:7-16: The surpassing worth of knowing Jesus.

1John 5:20: That we may know him who is true.

Book Reference: "The Way to God" by D.L. Moody. Available free on the internet.

****

Chapter 53
Stand Firm

For freedom Christ has set us free; stand firm therefore, and do not submit again to a yoke of slavery.   Galatians 5:1

Finally, be strong in the Lord and in the strength of his might. Put on the whole armor of God, that you may be able to stand against the schemes of the devil. For we do not wrestle against flesh and blood, but against the rulers, against the authorities, against the cosmic powers over this present darkness, against the spiritual forces of evil in the heavenly places. Therefore take up the whole armor of God, that you may be able to withstand in the evil day, and having done all, to stand firm. Stand therefore, having fastened on the belt of truth, and having put on the breastplate of righteousness, and, as shoes for your feet, having put on the readiness given by the gospel of peace. In all circumstances take up the shield of faith, with which you can extinguish all the flaming darts of the evil one; and take the helmet of salvation, and the sword of the Spirit, which is the word of God, praying at all times in the Spirit, with all prayer and supplication. To that end keep alert with all perseverance...   Ephesians 6:10-18

Scripture admonishes those who are saved to *"stand firm."* Note that the instruction is not to march and conquer, but to *stand*. Jesus has already conquered and won the victory (Colossians 2:8-15). We need to *stand firm* in that victory.

In Ephesians 6:13-18 (above), we are given a word picture of how we are to *stand firm*, with *the whole armor of God* for protection. This word picture shows us many of the provisions God has made for us to be victorious:

- *The belt of truth:* The main weapon of the devil and demons is lies. Knowing truth protects us from their lies. The main truth we know is that Jesus is the Christ, the Son of God, who died to redeem sinners; and who rose from the dead. Know the truth and stand firm in it!

- **The breastplate of righteousness:** Through Jesus' death and resurrection our sins are forgiven and we are made righteous before God (1John 1:9). Accusations to the contrary are false. Stand firm in the righteousness that is ours through Jesus! (Also see chapters 29, 30, 31, 32 and 42.)

- **Shoes... the readiness given by the gospel of peace:** We now have peace with God through Jesus (Romans 5:1). We should stand firm in that peace and be ready to share the good news, the gospel of peace, with others (1Peter 3:15).

- **The shield of faith:** Having firm faith in God and his promises enables us to **extinguish all the flaming darts of the evil one.** Stand firm in faith! (Also see chapter 35 "Faith.")

- **The helmet of salvation:** Nothing in all creation can separate us from God's love (Romans 8:31-39). Stand firm in the hope of salvation! (1Thessalonians 5:8)

- **The sword of the Spirit, which is the word of God:** We should know scripture and stand firm with it. Speak specific verses aloud to help you stand firm (Jesus shows us how in Matthew 4:1-11). Stand firm with the word of God!

- **Praying at all times in the Spirit:** We should always be in communication with God. Never stop praying! (1Thessalonians 5:17) (Also see chapter 24 *"Prayer."*)

- **Keep alert with all perseverance:** Standing firm requires that we always pay attention. As Jesus himself said: **"Be on guard! Be alert!"** (Mark 13:33 NIV)

Thank you God, for the victory that is ours as we stand firm in Jesus, with the whole armor of God!

For Further Reflection

Philippians 1:27-28: Standing firm in one spirit.

2Thessalonians 2:15: Stand firm.

Book Reference: "Sit, Walk, Stand" by Watchman Nee.

Book Reference: "The Overcoming Life" by D.L. Moody.

****

Conclusion

God is GOOD; ALL the time; in EVERY way!

Throughout this book we have seen God's goodness, his love and his grace for his people. Take hold of these truths! Do not let go of them! Consider reviewing this book in a few weeks or months, to remind yourself of these things.

> ***Do not merely listen to the word, and so deceive yourselves. Do what it says.***   James 1:22 NIV

As I did in the Introduction, I again encourage you to make the following prayer your own:

> *O God, help me to know your love for me.*
>
> *Help me to learn your ways, and to walk in them.*
>
> *Open my spiritual eyes to see myself as you see me, and to understand my circumstances as you understand them.*
>
> *Fill me with your Spirit so that I will be able to follow you wherever you lead.*

In closing:

> ***Now may the God of peace who brought again from the dead our Lord Jesus, the great shepherd of the sheep, by the blood of the eternal covenant, equip you with everything good that you may do his will, working in us that which is pleasing in his sight, through Jesus Christ, to whom be glory forever and ever. Amen.***
>
> Hebrews 13:20-21

> ***The Spirit and the bride say, "Come!" And let him who hears say, "Come!" Whoever is thirsty, let him come; and whoever wishes, let him take the free gift of the water of life.***   Revelation 22:17 NIV

> ***The grace of the Lord Jesus be with God's people. Amen.***   Revelation 22:21 NIV

****

Other Books by the Author

Beneath
Foundations for Eternal Life

Does *truth* exist? What is *truth*? How can *truth* be known? Through observation and reason many aspects of *truth* can be known. These kinds of *truths* form the bedrock on which true faith and knowledge can be built. Consider for yourself whether or not you agree that the *"truths"* discussed in this book are *"self-evident"*!

Building on
Foundations for Eternal Life

King Solomon wrote: *"Blessed are those who find wisdom, those who gain understanding, for she is more profitable than silver and yields better returns than gold. She is more precious than rubies; nothing you desire can compare with her."* (Proverbs 3:13-15 NIV)

"Nothing you desire can compare with her." Do you have it? Is it really that valuable? Do you have *wisdom* and *understanding*?

Free ebook versions of these books should be available at:

ShalomKoinonia.org

* * * * * * * * * * *

Made in the USA
Columbia, SC
13 February 2023